Welcome to Classic Weekend, the eighth brochure in the RYC Classic Collection. It features a collection of Aran-weight handknits inspired by a winter weekend spent in a cottage by the sea. The design emphasis is on easy-to-wear but stylish comfort, cosy textures and warming colours.

Shot on location in and around a traditional stone croft, built to keep out the wild Scottish weather, our Classic Weekend collection reflects the surroundings of the rugged northern coastline with its rocky shores, sea and lichen hues, and windswept lines.

Designs include ribs and cables inspired by traditional knitwear patterns, and stripes and squares in colours of sea and shore. The accent is firmly simple, cosy shapes that can be worn with jeans. Clever detailing – a big, floppy collar or a deep v-neck – adds a touch of individuality.

To accompany this beautiful brochure is a new yarn for the season. Cashsoft Aran is a velvety, cosy cashmere/wool blend, available in a range of beautiful, soft colours, including Bud green, Burst red, Foxglove lilac and Haze blue.

Martin

CLASSICweekend

15 designs in **Cashsoft Aran**

by Martin Storey

In our ever-pressured world, time has become the greatest luxury. And nothing is more precious than free time – time for enjoyment, time for ourselves. Weekends are an opportunity to get away from the rush of the week, to be outdoors. The Scottish highlands and islands are the ultimate escape!

 8 | **Harris**
Cashsoft Aran

 10 | **Paisley**
Cashsoft Aran

 14 | **Faeroe**
Cashsoft Aran

 16 | **Dundee**
Cashsoft Aran

 28 | **Bonnie bag**
Cashsoft Aran

 31 | **Tammy beret & mittens**
Cashsoft Aran

 33 | **Bonnie blanket**
Cashsoft Aran

 34 | **Bonnie scarf**
Cashsoft Aran

Knitted in Cashsoft Aran, shown here in Oat. Pattern instructions page 74

Harris – This cape is softly enveloping and wonderfully cosy. An updated classic for the coming season, its feminine touch makes it look good for day or evening.

Knitted in Cashsoft Aran, shown here in Mole. Pattern instructions page 54

Paisley – A big rib collar is the distinctive feature of our soft and cosy cardigan coat with its tie belt. Wrap up warm for a wintry day and keep out the cold north wind.

Knitted in Cashsoft Aran, shown here in Foxglove. Pattern instructions page 56

Faeroe *(shown here with Dundee)* – The far-flung Faeroe islands inspired this cabled jumper with its subtle surface which echoes the patterning made by the ebb and flow of the sea on the sand.

Knitted in Cashsoft Aran, shown here in Burst [Dundee], Kale [Tammy beret], Kale & Burst [Tammy mittens]. Pattern instructions page 71, 53 & 52

Dundee *(shown here with Tammy beret)* – This cabled zip-up keeps out all weathers and is ideal for a walk by the sea – followed by a slice of famous Dundee cake, a rich fruit cake that takes its name from the Scottish city.

Tammy mittens – Don't forget your mittens. These are extra long to keep your wrists warm and the icy wind out!

Knitted in Cashsoft Aran, shown here in Haze. Pattern instructions page 50

Rona – This soft wrap-over has a cap sleeve and moss stitch detailing. Wear it over a soft long-sleeved shirt with pyjama bottoms and just relax!

Knitted in Cashsoft Aran, shown here in Mole. Pattern instructions page 62

Nessie – Sorry, we couldn't resist calling this slipover Nessie. Its deep v-neck and easy shape make it ideal for pulling on over a pair of pyjamas to sit by the fire.

Knitted in Cashsoft Aran, shown here in Bud. Pattern instructions page 66

Katrine – The big collar, with a zip detail, makes this sweater a stylish choice to wear for strolling along the beach with a camera. Katrine is a northern variation of the name Katharine.

Knitted in Cashsoft Aran, shown here in Oat, Foxglove, Mole, Haze, Burst, Bud, Kale & Tornado. Pattern instructions page 70

Bonnie bag *(shown here with Katrine)* – Stow your thermos of hot chocolate in this boho patchwork bag and head for a hike in the hills.

Knitted in Cashsoft Aran, shown opposite in Kale, Foxglove [Tammy beret] & Kale [Tammy mittens]. Pattern instructions page 53 &52

Tammy Beret *(shown opposite with Tammy mittens)* – A tam-o-shanter or tammy is a Scottish beret, sometimes with a pom-pom or feather in the centre. Our version is perfect for the bonnie lassie who loves the great outdoors.

Bonnie blanket –
This trendy granny-
square blanket will
become your best pal,
whether by the fire-side
or on the beach.
Granny knows best
when it comes to
keeping warm!

Knitted in Cashsoft Aran, shown
here in Oat, Foxglove, Mole, Haze,
Burst, Bud, Kale & Tornado.
Pattern instructions page 68

Bonnie scarf –
Patchwork is back in
fashion for long
geometric scarves,
seen here knitted up in
our palette of Cashsoft
Aran colours.

Knitted in Cashsoft Aran, shown
here in Oat, Foxglove, Mole, Haze,
Burst, Bud, Kale & Tornado.
Pattern instructions page 69

Thistle – The purple thistle
has been the emblem
of Scotland since the
13th century. It was the
inspiration for this jacket
with a fashionable scarf
neck and knotted fringe
detail. Nothing prickly
about this though!

Knitted in Cashsoft Aran, shown here in
Kale. Pattern instructions page 58

Knitted in Cashsoft Aran, shown here in Tornado. Pattern instructions page 60

Highland – Gilets are perfect for outdoor activities and St Andrews is the world's most famous golf course.
Let's see, was that a hole-in-one?

Knitted in Cashsoft Aran, shown here in Mole & Oat. Pattern instructions page 63

Skye – This belted cardigan draws on the fairisle knitting tradition. Wear it for a winter picnic on the beach or even to row over the sea to Skye.

Cashsoft Aran
Oat

HARRIS

RONA

Cashsoft Aran
Haze

TAMMY MITTENS

TAMMY BERET

Tension

Obtaining the correct tension is perhaps the single factor which can make the difference between a successful garment and a disastrous one. It controls both the shape and size of an article, so any variation, however slight, can distort the finished garment. Different designers feature in our books and it is **their** tension, given at the **start** of each pattern, which you must match. We recommend that you knit a square in pattern and/or stocking stitch (depending on the pattern instructions) of perhaps 5 - 10 more stitches and 5 - 10 more rows than those given in the tension note. Mark out the central 10cm square with pins. If you have too many stitches to 10cm try again using thicker needles, if you have too few stitches to 10cm try again using finer needles. Once you have achieved the correct tension your garment will be knitted to the measurements indicated in the size diagram shown at the end of the pattern.

Sizing and Size Diagram Note

The instructions are given for the smallest size. Where they vary, work the figures in brackets for the larger sizes. **One set of figures refers to all sizes**. Included with most patterns in this magazine is a 'size diagram', or sketch of the finished garment and its dimensions. The size diagram shows the finished width of the garment at the under-arm point, and it is this measurement that the knitter should choose first; a useful tip is to measure one of your own garments which is a comfortable fit. Having chosen a size based on width, look at the corresponding length for that size; if you are not happy with the total length which we recommend, adjust your own garment before beginning your armhole shaping - any adjustment after this point will mean that your sleeve will not fit into your garment easily - don't forget to take your adjustment into account if there is any side seam shaping. Finally, look at the sleeve length; the size diagram shows the finished sleeve measurement, taking into account any top-arm insertion length. Measure your body between the centre of your neck and your wrist, this measurement should correspond to half the garment width plus the sleeve length. Again, your sleeve length may be adjusted, but remember to take into consideration your sleeve increases if you do adjust the length - you must increase more frequently than the pattern states to shorten your sleeve, less frequently to lengthen it.

Chart Note

Many of the patterns in the book are worked from charts. Each square on a chart represents a stitch and each line of squares a row of knitting. Each colour used is given a different letter and these are shown in the **materials** section, or in the **key**

alongside the chart of each pattern. When working from the charts, read odd rows (K) from right to left and even rows (P) from left to right, unless otherwise stated.

Knitting with colour

There are two main methods of working colour into a knitted fabric: **Intarsia** and **Fairisle** techniques. The first method produces a single thickness of fabric and is usually used where a colour is only required in a particular area of a row and does not form a repeating pattern across the row, as in the fairisle technique.

Intarsia: The simplest way to do this is to cut short lengths of yarn for each motif or block of colour used in a row. Then joining in the various colours at the appropriate point on the row, link one colour to the next by twisting them around each other where they meet on the wrong side to avoid gaps. All ends can then either be darned along the colour join lines, as each motif is completed or then can be "knitted-in" to the fabric of the knitting as each colour is worked into the pattern. This is done in much the same way as "weaving-in" yarns when working the Fairisle technique and does save time darning-in ends. It is essential that the tension is noted for **Intarsia** as this may vary from the stocking stitch if both are used in the same pattern.

Fairisle type knitting: When two or three colours are worked repeatedly across a row, strand the yarn **not** in use loosely behind the stitches being worked. If you are working with more than two colours, treat the "floating" yarns as if they were one yarn and always spread the stitches to their correct width to keep them elastic. It is advisable not to carry the stranded or "floating" yarns over more than three stitches at a time, but to weave them under and over the colour you are working. The "floating" yarns are therefore caught at the back of the work.

Finishing Instructions

After working for hours knitting a garment, it seems a great pity that many garments are spoiled because such little care is taken in the pressing and finishing process. Follow the following tips for a truly professional-looking garment.

Pressing

Block out each piece of knitting and following the instructions on the ball band press the garment pieces, omitting the ribs. Tip: Take special care to press the edges, as this will make sewing up both easier and neater. If the ball band indicates that the fabric is not to be pressed, then covering the blocked out fabric with a damp white cotton cloth and leaving it to stand will have the desired effect. Darn in all ends neatly along the selvage edge or a colour join, as appropriate.

Stitching

When stitching the pieces together, remember to match areas of colour and texture very carefully where they meet. Use a seam stitch such as back stitch or mattress stitch for all main knitting seams and join all ribs and neckband with mattress stitch, unless otherwise stated.

Construction

Having completed the pattern instructions, join left shoulder and neckband seams as detailed above. Sew the top of the sleeve to the body of the garment using the method detailed in the pattern, referring to the appropriate guide:

Set-in sleeves: Place centre of cast-off edge of sleeve to shoulder seam.
Set in sleeve, easing sleeve head into armhole.

Join side and sleeve seams.
Slip stitch pocket edgings and linings into place.
Sew on buttons to correspond with buttonholes.
Ribbed welts and neckbands and any area of garter stitch should not be pressed.

Abbreviations

K	knit	WS	wrong side
P	purl	sl 1	slip one stitch
st(s)	stitch(es)	psso	pass slipped
inc	increase(e)(ing)		stitch over
dec	decrease(e)(ing)	tbl	through back
st st	stocking stitch		of loop
	(1 row K, 1 row P)	M1	make one stitch
g st	garter stitch		by picking up
	(K every row)		horizontal loop
beg	begin(ning)		before next stitch
foll	following		and working into
rem	remain(ing)		back of it
rep	repeat	yrn	yarn round
alt	alternate		needle
cont	continue	meas	measures
patt	pattern	o	no stitches, times
tog	together		or rows
mm	millimetres	-	no stitches,
cm	centimetres		times or rows for
in(s)	inch(es)		that size
RS	right side	approx	approximately

 = Easy, straight forward knitting

 = Suitable for the average knitter

 = For the more experienced knitter

YARN

	XS	S	M	L	XL	
To fit bust	81	86	91	97	102	cm
	32	34	36	38	40	in
RYC Cashsoft Aran						
	8	9	9	10	10	x 50gm

(photographed in Haze 004)

NEEDLES

1 pair 4mm (no 8) (US 6) needles
1 pair 4½mm (no 7) (US 7) needles
4mm (no 8) (US 6) circular needle
2 double-pointed 4mm (no 8) (US 6) needles
Cable needle

TENSION

19 sts and 25 rows to 10 cm measured over stocking stitch using 4½mm (US 7) needles.

SPECIAL ABBREVIATIONS

C2B = slip next st onto cable needle and leave at back of work, K1, then K1 from cable needle;
C2F = slip next st onto cable needle and leave at front of work, K1, then K1 from cable needle;
C4B = slip next 3 sts onto cable needle and leave at back of work, K1, then K3 from cable needle;
C4F = slip next st onto cable needle and leave at front of work, K3, then K1 from cable needle.

BACK

Using 4mm (US 6) needles cast on 83 [87: 93: 97: 103] sts.
Row 1 (RS): K0 [0: 0: 0: 2], P1 [3: 0: 2: 3], *K3, P3, rep from * to last 4 [0: 3: 5: 2] sts, K3 [0: 3: 3: 2], P1 [0: 0: 2: 0].
Row 2: P0 [0: 0: 0: 2], K1 [3: 0: 2: 3], *P3, K3, rep from * to last 4 [0: 3: 5: 2] sts, P3 [0: 3: 3: 2], K1 [0: 0: 2: 0].
These 2 rows form rib.
Work in rib for a further 3 rows, ending with **WS** facing for next row.
Row 6 (WS): Rib 16 [18: 21: 23: 26], M1, (rib 1, M1) 4 times, rib 43, M1, (rib 1, M1) 4 times, rib to end. 93 [97: 103: 107: 113] sts.
Change to 4½mm (US 7) needles.
Row 1 (RS): P1 [1: 0: 0: 1], (K1, P1) 3 [4: 6: 7: 8] times, K1, P2, C2B, C2F, P2, K9, P2, C2B, C2F, P2, (K1, P1) 13 times, K1, P2, C2B, C2F, P2, K9, P2,

C2B, C2F, P2, K1, (P1, K1) 3 [4: 6: 7: 8] times, P1 [1: 0: 0: 1].
Row 2: K1 [1: 0: 0: 1], (P1, K1) 3 [4: 6: 7: 8] times, P1, K2, P4, K2, P9, K2, P4, K2, (P1, K1) 13 times, P1, K2, P4, K2, P9, K2, P4, K2, P1, (K1, P1) 3 [4: 6: 7: 8] times, K1 [1: 0: 0: 1].
Row 3 K1 [1: 0: 0: 1], (P1, K1) 3 [4: 6: 7: 8] times, K1, P2, C2F, C2B, P2, C4B, K1, C4F, P2, C2F, C2B, P2, K2, (P1, K1) 12 times, K1, P2, C2F, C2B, P2, C4B, K1, C4F, P2, C2F, C2B, P2, K1, (P1, K1) 3 [4: 6: 7: 8] times, K1 [1: 0: 0: 1].
Row 4: P1 [1: 0: 0: 1], (K1, P1) 3 [4: 6: 7: 8] times, P1, K2, P4, K2, P9, K2, P4, K2, P2, (K1, P1) 12 times, P1, K2, P4, K2, P9, K2, P4, K2, P1, (P1, K1) 3 [4: 6: 7: 8] times, P1 [1: 0: 0: 1].
These 4 rows form patt.
Cont in patt, dec 1 st at each end of 9th [11th: 11th: 13th: 13th] and every foll 6th row to 87 [91: 97: 101: 107] sts, then on every foll 4th row until 83 [87: 93: 97: 103] sts rem.
Work 9 rows, ending with RS facing for next row.
Inc 1 st at each end of next and every foll 6th row to 91 [95: 101: 105: 111] sts, then on foll 8th row. 93 [97: 103: 107: 113] sts.
Work 7 rows, ending with RS facing for next row. (Back should meas 32 [33: 33: 34: 34] cm.)
Shape raglan armholes
Keeping patt correct, cast off 5 sts at beg of next 2 rows. 83 [87: 93: 97: 103] sts.
Dec 1 st at each end of next 5 [7: 11: 13: 17] rows, then on every foll alt row until 23 [25: 25: 27: 27] sts rem.
Work 1 row, ending with RS facing for next row.
Cast off.

LEFT FRONT

Using 4mm (US 6) needles cast on 64 [66: 69: 71: 74] sts.
Row 1 (RS): K0 [0: 0: 0: 2], P1 [3: 0: 2: 3], *K3, P3, rep from * to last 3 sts, K3.
Row 2: *P3, K3, rep from * to last 4 [0: 3: 5: 2] sts, P3 [0: 3: 3: 2], K1 [0: 0: 2: 0].
These 2 rows form rib.
Work in rib for a further 3 rows, ending with **WS** facing for next row.
Row 6 (WS): Rib 44, M1, (rib 1, M1) 4 times, rib to end. 69 [71: 74: 76: 79] sts.
Change to 4½mm (US 7) needles.

Row 1 (RS): P1 [1: 0: 0: 1], (K1, P1) 3 [4: 6: 7: 8] times, K1, P2, C2B, C2F, P2, K9, P2, C2B, C2F, P2, (K1, P1) 18 times.
Row 2: K1, (P1, K1) 17 times, P1, K2, P4, K2, P9, K2, P4, K2, P1, (K1, P1) 3 [4: 6: 7: 8] times, K1 [1: 0: 0: 1].
Row 3 K1 [1: 0: 0: 1], (P1, K1) 3 [4: 6: 7: 8] times, K1, P2, C2F, C2B, P2, C4B, K1, C4F, P2, C2F, C2B, P2, K2, (P1, K1) 17 times.
Row 4: P1, (K1, P1) 17 times, P1, K2, P4, K2, P9, K2, P4, K2, P1, (P1, K1) 3 [4: 6: 7: 8] times, P1 [1: 0: 0: 1].
These 4 rows form patt.
Cont in patt, dec 1 st at beg of 9th [11th: 11th: 13th: 13th] and every foll 6th row to 66 [68: 71: 73: 76] sts, then on every foll 4th row until 64 [66: 69: 71: 74] sts rem.
Work 3 rows, ending with RS facing for next row.
Shape front slope
Keeping patt correct, dec 1 st at end of next and foll 19 alt rows **and at same time** inc 1 st at beg of 7th and 3 foll 6th rows, then on foll 8th row. 49 [51: 54: 56: 59] sts.
Work 1 row, ending with RS facing for next row. (Left front should now match back to beg of raglan armhole shaping.)
Shape raglan armhole
Keeping patt correct, cast off 5 sts at beg and dec 1 st at end of next row. 43 [45: 48: 50: 53] sts.
Work 1 row.
Dec 1 st at raglan armhole edge of next 5 [7: 11: 13: 17] rows, then on foll 23 [22: 21: 20: 19] alt rows **and at same time** dec 1 st at front slope edge on 3rd and 6 [9: 8: 11: 10] foll 4th rows, then on 4 [2: 3: 1: 2] foll 6th rows. 4 sts.
Dec 1 st at raglan armhole edge **only** on 2nd and foll alt row. 2 sts.
Work 1 row, ending with RS facing for next row.
Next row (RS): K2tog and fasten off.

RIGHT FRONT

Using 4mm (US 6) needles cast on 64 [66: 69: 71: 74] sts.
Row 1 (RS): *K3, P3, rep from * to last 4 [0: 3: 5: 2] sts, K3 [0: 3: 3: 2], P1 [0: 0: 2: 0].
Row 2: P0 [0: 0: 0: 2], K1 [3: 0: 2: 3], *P3, K3, rep from * to last 3 sts, P3.
These 2 rows form rib.

Work in rib for a further 3 rows, ending with **WS** facing for next row.

Row 6 (WS): Rib 16 [18: 21: 23: 26], M1, (rib 1, M1) 4 times, rib to end. 69 [71: 74: 76: 79] sts. Change to 4½mm (US 7) needles.

Row 1 (RS): (P1, K1) 18 times, P2, C2B, C2F, P2, K9, P2, C2B, C2F, P2, K1, (P1, K1) 3 [4: 6: 7: 8] times, P1 [1: 0: 0: 1].

Row 2: K1 [1: 0: 0: 1], (P1, K1) 3 [4: 6: 7: 8] times, P1, K2, P4, K2, P9, K2, P4, K2, (P1, K1) 18 times.

Row 3 K1, (P1, K1) 17 times, K1, P2, C2F, C2B, P2, C4B, K1, C4F, P2, C2F, C2B, P2, K1, (K1, P1) 3 [4: 6: 7: 8] times, K1 [1: 0: 0: 1].

Row 4: P1 [1: 0: 0: 1], (K1, P1) 3 [4: 6: 7: 8] times, P1, K2, P4, K2, P9, K2, P4, K2, P2, (K1, P1) 17 times.

These 4 rows form patt.

Cont in patt, dec 1 st at end of 9th [11th: 11th: 13th: 13th] and every foll 6th row to 66 [68: 71: 73: 76] sts, then on every foll 4th row until 64 [66: 69: 71: 74] sts rem.

Complete to match left front, reversing shapings, working an extra row before beg of raglan armhole shaping.

SLEEVES

Using 4mm (US 6) needles cast on 64 [64: 66: 66: 68] sts.

Row 1 (RS): Knit.

Row 2: K30 [30: 31: 31: 32], (M1, K1) 4 times, M1, K to end. 69 [69: 71: 71: 73] sts. Change to 4½mm (US 7) needles.

Shape raglan

Row 1 (RS): Cast off 5 sts (one st on right needle), P1 [1: 0: 0: 1], (K1, P1) 7 [7: 8: 8: 8] times, K1, P2, C2B, C2F, P2, K9, P2, C2B, C2F, P2, K1, (P1, K1) 10 [10: 11: 11: 11] times, P1 [1: 0: 0: 1].

Row 2: Cast off 5 sts (one st on right needle), K1 [1: 0: 0:1], (P1, K1) 7 [7: 8: 8: 8] times, P1, K2, P4, K2, P9, K2, P4, K2, P1, (K1, P1) 8 [8: 8: 8: 9] times, K0 [0: 1: 1: 0]. 59 [59: 61: 61: 63] sts.

Row 3: K0 [0: 1: 1: 0], (P1, K1) 8 [8: 8: 8: 9] times, K1, P2, C2F, C2B, P2, C4B, K1, C4F, P2, C2F, C2B, P2, K1, (K1, P1) 8 [8: 8: 8: 9] times, K0 [0: 1: 1: 0].

Row 4: P0 [0: 1: 1: 0], (K1, P1) 8 [8: 8: 8: 9] times, P1, K2, P4, K2, P9, K2, P4, K2, P1, (P1, K1) 8 [8: 8: 8: 9] times, P0 [0: 1: 1: 0].

Last 4 rows form patt.

Cont in patt, dec 1 st at each end of next and every foll alt row until 5 sts rem.

Work 1 row, ending with RS facing for next row.

Cast off rem 5 sts.

MAKING UP

Press as described on the information page. Join raglan seams using back stitch, or mattress stitch if preferred.

Front band

With RS facing and using 4mm (US 6) circular needle, beg and ending at cast-on edges, pick up and knit 33 [35: 35: 37: 37] sts up right front opening edge to beg of front slope shaping, 78 [78: 80: 80: 82] sts up right front slope, 5 sts from right sleeve, 23 [25: 25: 27: 27] sts from back, 5 sts from left sleeve, 78 [78: 80: 80: 82] sts down left front slope to beg of front slope shaping, then 33 [35: 35: 37: 37] sts down left front opening edge. 255 [261: 265: 271: 275] sts.

Work in g st for 2 rows, ending with **WS** facing for next row.

Cast off knitwise (on **WS**).

Right tie

Cast on 3 sts using double-pointed 4mm (US 6) needles.

Row 1 (RS): K3, *without turning slip these 3 sts to opposite end of needle and bring yarn to opposite end of work pulling it quite tightly across WS of work, K these 3 sts again, rep from * until tie is 31 cm long, K3tog and fasten off.

Left tie

Work as given for right tie, but working a strip 66 cm long.

See information page for finishing instructions, leaving a small opening in right side seam level with beg of front slope shaping. Attach ends of ties to cast-off edge of front border level with beg of front slope shaping.

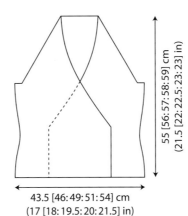

55 [56: 57: 58: 59] cm (21.5 [22: 22.5: 23: 23] in)

43.5 [46: 49: 51: 54] cm (17 [18: 19.5: 20: 21.5] in)

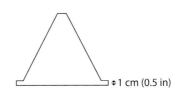

1 cm (0.5 in)

Tammy mittens

YARN

RYC Cashsoft Aran

Striped mittens

A	Kale	007	2	x 50gm
B	Burst	005	1	x 50gm

Plain mittens

	2	x 50gm

(photographed in Kale 007)

NEEDLES

1 pair 4mm (no 8) (US 6) needles
1 pair 4½mm (no 7) (US 7) needles

TENSION

19 sts and 25 rows to 10 cm measured over stocking stitch using 4½mm (US 7) needles.

Plain mittens

Work as given for striped mittens (below) but using same colour throughout.

Striped mittens

RIGHT MITTEN

Using 4mm (US 6) needles and yarn A cast on 39 sts.
Row 1 (RS): K1, *P1, K1, rep from * to end.
Row 2: P1, *K1, P1, rep from * to end.
These 2 rows form rib.
Work in rib for a further 6 rows, ending with RS facing for next row.
Change to 4½mm (US 7) needles.
Join in yarn B and, beg with a K row, cont in striped st st as folls:
Using yarn B, work 4 rows, dec 1 st at each end of first of these rows. 37 sts.
Using yarn A, work 4 rows.
These 8 rows form striped st st and beg shaping.
Cont in striped st st, dec 1 st at each end of 13th

and foll 18th row. 33 sts.
Work 1 row, ending after 4 rows using yarn A and with RS facing for next row.
Shape thumb gusset
Keeping stripes correct, cont as folls:
Row 1 (RS): K17, inc in next st, K1, inc in next st, K13. 35 sts.
Work 3 rows.
Row 5: K17, inc in next st, K3, inc in next st, K13. 37 sts.
Work 3 rows.
Row 9: K17, inc in next st, K5, inc in next st, K13. 39 sts.
Work 3 rows.
Row 13: K17, inc in next st, K7, inc in next st, K13. 41 sts.
Work 3 rows.
Row 17: K17, inc in next st, K9, inc in next st, K13. 43 sts.
Work 1 row.
Shape thumb
Next row (RS): K30 and turn.
****Next row:** Cast on and P 2 sts, P14 and turn.
Next row: Cast on and K 2 sts, K16.
Work a further 7 rows on these 18 sts only, ending after 4 rows using yarn B and with RS facing for next row.
Next row (RS): (K1, K2tog) 6 times. 12 sts.
Work 1 row.
Next row: (K2tog) 6 times.
Break yarn and thread through rem 6 sts. Pull up tight and fasten off securely. Sew thumb seam.
Rejoin yarn B at base of thumb, pick up and K 4 sts from cast-on edge of thumb, K to end. 33 sts.
Work 23 rows, ending after 2 rows using yarn B and with RS facing for next row.
Shape top
Row 1 (RS): K1, (K2tog, K1, K2tog tbl, K8) twice, K2tog, K1, K2tog tbl, K1. 27 sts.

Work 1 row.
Row 3: K1, (K2tog, K1, K2tog tbl, K5) twice, K2tog, K1, K2tog tbl, K1. 21 sts.
Work 1 row.
Row 5: K1, (K2tog, K1, K2tog tbl, K2) twice, K2tog, K1, K2tog tbl, K1.
Work 1 row.
Cast off rem 15 sts.

LEFT MITTEN

Work as given for right mitten to beg of thumb gusset shaping.
Shape thumb gusset
Keeping stripes correct, cont as folls:
Row 1 (RS): K13, inc in next st, K1, inc in next st, K17. 35 sts.
Work 3 rows.
Row 5: K13, inc in next st, K3, inc in next st, K17. 37 sts.
Work 3 rows.
Row 9: K13, inc in next st, K5, inc in next st, K17. 39 sts.
Work 3 rows.
Row 13: K13, inc in next st, K7, inc in next st, K17. 41 sts.
Work 3 rows.
Row 17: K13, inc in next st, K9, inc in next st, K17. 43 sts.
Work 1 row.
Shape thumb
Next row (RS): K27 and turn.
Complete as given for right mitten from **.

MAKING UP

Press as described on the information page.
Join side and top seam using back stitch, or mattress stitch if preferred.

Tammy beret

YARN
RYC Cashsoft Aran

Striped beret

A Kale	007	1	x 50gm
B Foxglove	002	1	x 50gm

Plain beret

		2	x 50gm

(photographed in Kale 007)

NEEDLES
1 pair 4mm (no 8) (US 6) needles
1 pair 4½mm (no 7) (US 7) needles

TENSION
19 sts and 25 rows to 10 cm measured over
stocking stitch using 4½mm (US 7) needles.

PLAIN BERET
Work as given for striped beret (below) but using
same colour throughout.

STRIPED BERET
Using 4mm (US 6) needles and yarn A cast on
99 sts.
Row 1 (RS): K1, *P1, K1, rep from * to end.
Row 2: P1, *K1, P1, rep from * to end.
These 2 rows form rib.
Work in rib for a further 5 rows, ending with WS
facing for next row.
Row 8 (WS): Rib 4, *M1, rib 2, rep from * to last
3 sts, rib 3. 145 sts.
Change to 4½mm (US 7) needles.

Join in yarn B and, beg with a K row, cont in
striped st st as folls:
Using yarn B, work 4 rows.
Using yarn A, work 4 rows.
These 8 rows form striped st st.
Cont in striped st st for a further 12 rows, ending
with RS facing for next row.
Shape top
Keeping stripes correct, cont as folls:
Row 1 (RS): *K6, K2tog, rep from * to last st, K1.
127 sts.
Work 3 rows.
Row 5: *K5, K2tog, rep from * to last st, K1. 109 sts.
Work 3 rows.
Row 9: *K4, K2tog, rep from * to last st, K1. 91 sts.
Work 3 rows.
Row 13: *K3, K2tog, rep from * to last st, K1. 73 sts.
Work 3 rows.
Row 17: *K2, K2tog, rep from * to last st, K1. 55 sts.
Work 3 rows.
Row 21: *K1, K2tog, rep from * to last st, K1. 37 sts.
Work 3 rows.
Row 25: *K2tog, rep from * to last st, K1. 19 sts.
Work 1 row.
Row 27: As row 25.
Break yarn and thread through rem 10 sts. Pull up
tight and fasten off securely.

MAKING UP
Press as described on the information page.
Join back seam using back stitch, or mattress
stitch if preferred.

Paisley

YARN

	XS	S	M	L	XL	
To fit bust	81	86	91	97	102	cm
	32	34	36	38	40	in

RYC Cashsoft Aran

	25	26	28	29	30 x 50gm

(photographed in Mole 003)

NEEDLES

1 pair 4mm (no 8) (US 6) needles
1 pair 4½mm (no 7) (US 7) needles

TENSION

19 sts and 25 rows to 10 cm measured over stocking stitch using 4½mm (US 7) needles.

BACK

Using 4mm (US 6) needles cast on 122 [130: 134: 142: 146] sts.
Row 1 (RS): K2, *P2, K2, rep from * to end.
Row 2: P2, *K2, P2, rep from * to end.
These 2 rows form rib.
Cont in rib for a further 29 rows, ending with **WS** facing for next row.
Row 32 (WS): Rib 9 [1: 9: 1: 9], work 2 tog, *rib 4, work 2 tog, rep from * to last 9 [1: 9: 1: 9] sts, rib to end.
104 [108: 114: 118: 124] sts.
Change to 4½mm (US 7) needles.
Beg with a K row, work in st st for 18 [20: 20: 22: 22] rows, ending with RS facing for next row.
Next row (dec) (RS): (K10 [10: 11: 11: 12], K2tog) twice, K to last 24 [24: 26: 26: 28] sts, (sl 1, K1, psso, K10 [10: 11: 11: 12]) twice.
Work 11 rows.
Rep last 12 rows twice more, then first of these rows (the dec row) again.
88 [92: 98: 102: 108] sts.
Cont straight until back meas 58 [59: 59: 60: 60] cm, ending with RS facing for next row.
Shape armholes
Cast off 5 [5: 6: 6: 7] sts at beg of next 2 rows.
78 [82: 86: 90: 94] sts.
Dec 1 st at each end of next 3 [3: 5: 5: 7] rows, then on foll 3 alt rows, then on every foll 4th row until 62 [64: 66: 68: 70] sts rem.
Cont straight until armhole meas 23 [23: 24: 24: 25] cm, ending with RS facing for next row.

Shape shoulders and back neck
Cast off 5 [5: 6: 6: 6] sts at beg of next 2 rows.
52 [54: 54: 56: 58] sts.
Next row (RS): Cast off 5 [5: 6: 6: 6] sts, K until there are 10 [10: 9: 9: 10] sts on right needle and turn, leaving rem sts on a holder.
Work each side of neck separately.
Cast off 4 sts at beg of next row.
Cast off rem 6 [6: 5: 5: 6] sts.
With RS facing, rejoin yarn to rem sts, cast off centre 22 [24: 24: 26: 26] sts, K to end.
Complete to match first side, reversing shapings.

LEFT FRONT

Using 4mm (US 6) needles cast on 95 [99: 103: 103: 107] sts.
Row 1 (RS): *K2, P2, rep from * to last 3 sts, K3.
Row 2: sl 1 purlwise, P2, *K2, P2, rep from * to end.
These 2 rows form rib.
Cont in rib for a further 29 rows, ending with **WS** facing for next row.
Row 32 (WS): Rib 35 and slip these sts onto a holder, rib 8 [4: 3: 9: 8], work 2 tog, *rib 4, work 2 tog, rep from * to last 8 [4: 3: 9: 8] sts, rib to end. 52 [54: 57: 59: 62] sts.
Change to 4½mm (US 7) needles.
Beg with a K row, work in st st for 18 [20: 20: 22: 22] rows, ending with RS facing for next row.
Next row (dec) (RS): (K10 [10: 11: 11: 12], K2tog) twice, K to end.
Work 11 rows.
Rep last 12 rows twice more, then first of these rows (the dec row) again. 44 [46: 49: 51: 54] sts.
Cont straight until left front matches back to beg of armhole shaping, ending with RS facing for next row.
Shape armhole
Cast off 5 [5: 6: 6: 7] sts at beg of next row.
39 [41: 43: 45: 47] sts.
Work 1 row.
Dec 1 st at armhole edge of next 3 [3: 5: 5: 7] rows, then on foll 3 alt rows, then on every foll 4th row until 31 [32: 33: 34: 35] sts rem.
Cont straight until 15 [15: 15: 17: 17] rows less have been worked than on back to beg of shoulder shaping, ending with **WS** facing for next row.

Shape neck
Cast off 7 [8: 8: 8: 8] sts at beg of next row.
24 [24: 25: 26: 27] sts.
Dec 1 st at neck edge of next 4 rows, then on foll 3 [3: 3: 4: 4] alt rows, then on foll 4th row, ending with RS facing for next row.
16 [16: 17: 17: 18] sts.
Shape shoulder
Cast off 5 [5: 6: 6: 6] sts at beg of next and foll alt row.
Work 1 row.
Cast off rem 6 [6: 5: 5: 6] sts.

RIGHT FRONT

Using 4mm (US 6) needles cast on 95 [99: 103: 103: 107] sts.
Row 1 (RS): sl 1 knitwise, K2, *P2, K2, rep from * to end.
Row 2: P2, *K2, P2, rep from * to last st, K1.
These 2 rows form rib.
Cont in rib for a further 29 rows, ending with **WS** facing for next row.
Row 32 (WS): Rib 8 [4: 3: 9: 8], work 2 tog, *rib 4, work 2 tog, rep from * to last 43 [39: 38: 44: 43] sts, rib 8 [4: 3: 9: 8] and turn, leaving rem 35 sts on a holder. 52 [54: 57: 59: 62] sts.
Change to 4½mm (US 7) needles.
Beg with a K row, work in st st for 18 [20: 20: 22: 22] rows, ending with RS facing for next row.
Next row (dec) (RS): K to last 24 [24: 26: 26: 28] sts, (sl 1, K1, psso, K10 [10: 11: 11: 12]) twice.
Complete to match left front, reversing shapings, working an extra row before beg of armhole, neck and shoulder shaping.

SLEEVES

Using 4mm (US 6) needles cast on 62 [62: 62: 66: 66] sts.
Work in rib as given for back for 32 rows, ending with RS facing for next row.
Change to 4½mm (US 7) needles.
Beg with a K row, cont in st st, shaping sides by inc 1 st at each end of 23rd [23rd: 13th: 25th: 13th] and every foll 26th [26th: 16th: 26th: 16th] row until there are 68 [68: 72: 72: 76] sts.
Cont straight until sleeve meas 48 [48: 49: 49: 49] cm, ending with RS facing for next row.

Shape top

Cast off 5 [5: 6: 6: 7] sts at beg of next 2 rows.
58 [58: 60: 60: 62] sts.
Dec 1 st at each end of next 3 rows, then on foll 3 alt rows, then on every foll 4th row until 42 [42: 44: 44: 46] sts rem.
Work 1 row, ending with RS facing for next row.
Dec 1 st at each end of next and every foll alt row to 34 sts, then on foll 7 rows, ending with RS facing for next row.
Cast off rem 20 sts.

MAKING UP

Press as described on the information page.
Join shoulder seams using back stitch, or mattress stitch if preferred.

Left front band

Slip 35 sts from left front holder onto 4mm (US 6) needles and rejoin yarn with RS facing.
Cont in rib as set until left front band, when slightly stretched, fits up left front opening edge to neck shaping, ending with RS facing for next row.
Break yarn and leave sts on a holder.
Slip stitch band in place.

Right front band

Slip 35 sts from right front holder onto 4mm (US 6) needles and rejoin yarn with **WS** facing.
Cont in rib as set until right front band, when slightly stretched, fits up right front opening edge to neck shaping, ending with RS facing for next row.
When band is complete, do NOT break yarn.
Slip stitch band in place.

Collar

With RS facing and using 4mm (US 6) needles, rib 35 sts of right front band, pick up and knit 25 [26: 26: 27: 29] sts up right side of neck, 32 [34: 34: 36: 36] sts from back, and 25 [26: 26: 27: 29] sts down left side of neck, then rib 35 sts of left front band.
152 [156: 156: 160: 164] sts.
Work in rib as set by bands for 5 cm.
Change to 4½mm (US 7) needles.
Cont in rib until collar meas 30 cm.
Cast off in rib.

Belt

Using 4mm (US 6) needles cast on 24 sts.
Row 1 (RS): sl 1 knitwise, (K2, P2) 5 times, K3.
Row 2: sl 1 purlwise, (P2, K2) 5 times, P2, K1.
Rep these 2 rows until belt meas 230 cm.
Cast off in rib.
Cut 30 cm lengths of yarn and knot groups of 6 of these lengths through cast-on and cast-off edges of belt, placing 6 evenly spaced knots across each end.
See information page for finishing instructions, setting in sleeves using the set-in method.

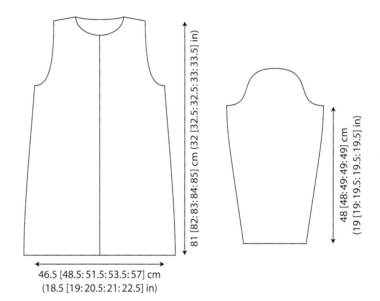

81 [82: 83: 84: 85] cm (32 [32.5: 32.5: 33: 33.5] in)

48 [48: 49: 49: 49] cm (19 [19: 19.5: 19.5: 19.5] in)

46.5 [48.5: 51.5: 53.5: 57] cm
(18.5 [19: 20.5: 21: 22.5] in)

YARN

	XS	S	M	L	XL
To fit bust	81	86	91	97	102 cm
	32	34	36	38	40 in

RYC Cashsoft Aran

| | 16 | 16 | 17 | 18 | 19 x 50gm |

(photographed in Foxglove 002)

NEEDLES

1 pair 4mm (no 8) (US 6) needles
1 pair 4½mm (no 7) (US 7) needles
Cable needle

TENSION

19 sts and 25 rows to 10 cm measured over stocking stitch using 4½mm (US 7) needles.

SPECIAL ABBREVIATIONS

C4B = slip next 2 sts onto cable needle and leave at back of work, K2, then K2 from cable needle; **Cr4R** = slip next st onto cable needle and leave at back of work, K3, then P1 from cable needle; **Cr4L** = slip next 3 sts onto cable needle and leave at front of work, P1, then K3 from cable needle; **Cr6R** = slip next 3 sts onto cable needle and leave at back of work, K3, then P3 from cable needle; **Cr6L** = slip next 3 sts onto cable needle and leave at front of work, P3, then K3 from cable needle; **C6B** = slip next 3 sts onto cable needle and leave at back of work, K3, then K3 from cable needle; **C6F** = slip next 3 sts onto cable needle and leave at front of work, K3, then K3 from cable needle.

BACK

Using 4mm (US 6) needles cast on 112 [116: 122: 126: 132] sts.
Row 1 (RS): K0 [0: 3: 0: 0], P0 [1: 1: 0: 1], K1 [2: 2: 0: 2], *P1, K4, P1, K2, rep from * to last 7 [1: 4: 6: 1] sts, P1, K4 [0: 3: 4: 0], P1 [0: 0: 1: 0], K1 [0: 0: 0: 0].
Row 2: P0 [0: 3: 0: 0], K0 [1: 1: 0: 1], P1 [2: 2: 0: 2], *K1, P4, K1, P2, rep from * to last 7 [1: 4: 6: 1] sts, K1, P4 [0: 3: 4: 0], K1 [0: 0: 1: 0], P1 [0: 0: 0: 0].
Row 3: K0 [0: 3: 0: 0], P0 [1: 1: 0: 1], K1 [2: 2: 0: 2], *P1, C4B, P1, K2, rep from * to last 7 [1: 4: 6: 1] sts, P1, (C4B) 1 [0: 0: 1: 0] times, K0 [0: 3: 0: 0], P1 [0: 0: 1: 0], K1 [0: 0: 0: 0].
Row 4: As row 2.

These 4 rows form cabled rib.
Cont in cabled rib for a further 23 rows, ending with **WS** facing for next row.
Row 28 (WS): Rib 39 [41: 44: 46: 49], (M1, rib 2, M1, rib 14) twice, M1, rib 2, M1, rib to end. 118 [122: 128: 132: 138] sts.
Change to 4½mm (US 7) needles.
Beg and ending rows as indicated and repeating the 32 row patt repeat throughout, cont in patt from chart for body as folls:
Cont straight until back meas 42 [43: 43: 44: 44] cm, ending with RS facing for next row.
Shape armholes
Keeping patt correct, cast off 5 [6: 6: 7: 7] sts at beg of next 2 rows. 108 [110: 116: 118: 124] sts.
Dec 1 st at each end of next 5 [5: 7: 7: 9] rows, then on foll 5 alt rows, then on foll 4th row. 86 [88: 90: 92: 94] sts.
Cont straight until armhole meas 22 [22: 23: 23: 24] cm, ending with RS facing for next row.
Shape shoulders and back neck
Cast off 7 [7: 7: 7: 8] sts at beg of next 2 rows. 72 [74: 76: 78: 78] sts.
Next row (RS): Cast off 7 [7: 7: 7: 8] sts, patt until there are 11 [11: 12: 12: 11] sts on right needle and turn, leaving rem sts on a holder.
Work each side of neck separately.
Cast off 4 sts at beg of next row.
Cast off rem 7 [7: 8: 8: 7] sts.
With RS facing, rejoin yarn to rem sts, cast off centre 36 [38: 38: 40: 40] sts dec 10 sts evenly, patt to end.
Complete to match first side, reversing shapings.

FRONT

Work as given for back until 16 [16: 16: 18: 18] rows less have been worked than on back to beg of shoulder shaping, ending with RS facing for next row.
Shape neck
Next row (RS): Patt 30 [30: 31: 32: 33] sts and turn, leaving rem sts on a holder.
Work each side of neck separately.
Keeping patt correct, dec 1 st at neck edge of next 5 rows, then on foll 3 [3: 3: 4: 4] alt rows, then on foll 4th row, ending with RS facing for next row. 21 [21: 22: 22: 23] sts.
Shape shoulder
Cast off 7 [7: 7: 7: 8] sts at beg of next and foll

alt row.
Work 1 row.
Cast off rem 7 [7: 8: 8: 7] sts.
With RS facing, rejoin yarn to rem sts, cast off centre 26 [28: 28: 28: 28] sts dec 7 sts evenly, patt to end.
Complete to match first side, reversing shapings.

SLEEVES

Using 4mm (US 6) needles cast on 52 [52: 54: 56: 56] sts.
Row 1 (RS): K0 [0: 1: 2: 2], P1, K2, *P1, K4, P1, K2, rep from * to last 1 [1: 2: 3: 3] sts, P1, K0 [0: 1: 2: 2].
Row 2: P0 [0: 1: 2: 2], K1, P2, *K1, P4, K1, P2, rep from * to last 1 [1: 2: 3: 3] sts, K1, P0 [0: 1: 2: 2].
Row 3: K0 [0: 1: 2: 2], P1, K2, *P1, C4B, P1, K2, rep from * to last 1 [1: 2: 3: 3] sts, P1, K0 [0: 1: 2: 2].
Row 4: As row 2.
These 4 rows form cabled rib.
Cont in cabled rib for a further 24 rows, ending with RS facing for next row.
Change to 4½mm (US 7) needles.
Beg and ending rows as indicated and repeating the 32 row patt repeat throughout, cont in patt from chart for sleeve, shaping sides by inc 1 st at each end of next and every foll 8th [6th: 6th: 6th: 6th] row to 74 [62: 62: 64: 72] sts, then on every foll - [8th: 8th: 8th: 8th] row until there are - [76: 78: 80: 82] sts, taking inc sts into double moss st.
Cont straight until sleeve meas 46 [46: 47: 47: 47] cm, ending with RS facing for next row.
Shape top
Keeping patt correct, cast off 5 [6: 6: 7: 7] sts at beg of next 2 rows. 64 [64: 66: 66: 68] sts.
Dec 1 st at each end of next 3 rows, then on foll 2 alt rows, then on every foll 4th row until 48 [48: 50: 50: 52] sts rem.
Work 1 row, ending with RS facing for next row.
Dec 1 st at each end of next and every foll alt row to 36 sts, then on foll 5 rows, ending with RS facing for next row.
Cast off rem 26 sts, dec 8 sts evenly.

MAKING UP

Press as described on the information page.
Join right shoulder seam using back stitch, or mattress stitch if preferred.
Neckband
With RS facing and using 4mm (US 6) needles,

pick up and knit 22 [22: 22: 24: 24] sts down left side of neck, 24 sts from front, 22 [22: 22: 24: 24] sts up right side of neck, then 38 [38: 38: 42: 42] sts from back.

106 [106: 106: 114: 114] sts.

Row 1 (WS): P2, *K1, P4, K1, P2, rep from * to end.
Row 2: K2, *P1, C4B, P1, K2, rep from * to end.
Row 3: As row 1.
Row 4: K2, *P1, K4, P1, K2, rep from * to end.
These 4 rows form cabled rib.
Cont in cabled rib for a further 19 rows, ending after patt row 3 and with RS facing for next row.
Cast off in rib.
See information page for finishing instructions, setting in sleeves using the set-in method.

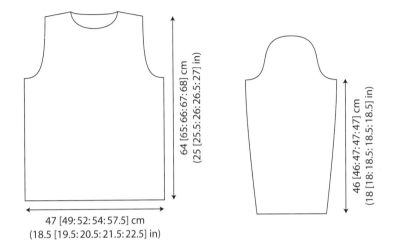

64 [65: 66: 67: 68] cm
(25 [25.5: 26: 26.5: 27] in)

47 [49: 52: 54: 57.5] cm
(18.5 [19.5: 20.5: 21.5: 22.5] in)

46 [46: 47: 47: 47] cm
(18 [18: 18.5: 18.5: 18.5] in)

Body chart

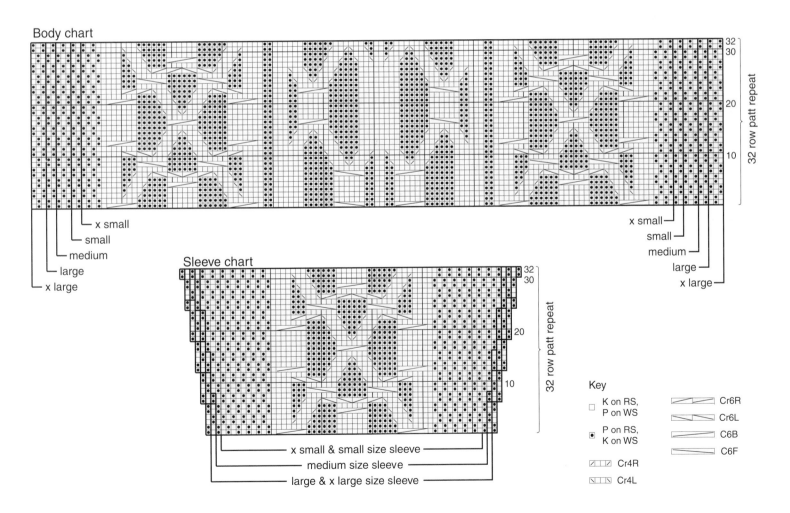

32 row patt repeat

x small
small
medium
large
x large

x small
small
medium
large
x large

Sleeve chart

32 row patt repeat

x small & small size sleeve
medium size sleeve
large & x large size sleeve

Key

☐ K on RS, P on WS

▣ P on RS, K on WS

⧄ Cr4R

⧅ Cr4L

⧄ Cr6R

⧅ Cr6L

▱ C6B

▱ C6F

Thistle

YARN

	XS	S	M	L	XL	
To fit bust	81	86	91	97	102	cm
	32	34	36	38	40	in
RYC Cashsoft Aran						
	21	22	23	24	25	x 50gm

(photographed in Kale 007)

NEEDLES

1 pair 4mm (no 8) (US 6) needles
1 pair 4½mm (no 7) (US 7) needles
2 double-pointed 4mm (no 8) (US 6) needles

TENSION

19 sts and 25 rows to 10 cm measured over stocking stitch using 4½mm (US 7) needles.

BACK

Using 4mm (US 6) needles cast on 105 [109: 115: 119: 125] sts.
Work in g st for 8 rows, ending with RS facing for next row.
Change to 4½mm (US 7) needles.
Beg with a K row, work in st st for 12 rows, ending with RS facing for next row.
Next row (dec) (RS): (K10 [10: 11: 11: 12], K2tog) twice, K to last 24 [24: 26: 26: 28] sts, (sl 1, K1, psso, K10 [10: 11: 11: 12]) twice.
Work 11 rows.
Rep last 12 rows twice more, then first of these rows (the dec row) again.
89 [93: 99: 103: 109] sts.
Cont straight until back meas 35 [36: 36: 37: 37] cm, ending with RS facing for next row.
Shape raglan armholes
Cast off 2 sts at beg of next 2 rows.
85 [89: 95: 99: 105] sts.
XL only
Next row (RS): K1, sl 1, K1, psso, K to last 3 sts, K2tog, K1.
Next row: K1, P2tog, P to last 3 sts, P2tog tbl, K1.
101 sts.
XS, S, M and L only
Next row (RS): K1, sl 1, K1, psso, K to last 3 sts, K2tog, K1.
Next row: K1, P to last st, K1.
Next row: Knit.
Next row: K1, P to last st, K1.

Rep last 4 rows 4 [3: 1: 0: -] times more.
75 [81: 91: 97: -] sts.
All sizes
Next row (RS): K1, sl 1, K1, psso, K to last 3 sts, K2tog, K1.
Next row: K1, P to last st, K1.
Rep last 2 rows 23 [25: 30: 32: 34] times more.
Cast off rem 27 [29: 29: 31: 31] sts.

LEFT FRONT

Using 4mm (US 6) needles cast on 53 [55: 58: 60: 63] sts.
Work in g st for 8 rows, ending with RS facing for next row.
Change to 4½mm (US 7) needles.
Beg with a K row, work in st st for 12 rows, ending with RS facing for next row.
Next row (dec) (RS): (K10 [10: 11: 11: 12], K2tog) twice, K to end.
Work 11 rows.
Rep last 12 rows twice more, then first of these rows (the dec row) again.
45 [47: 50: 52: 55] sts.
Cont straight until 12 rows less have been worked than on back to beg of raglan armhole shaping, ending with RS facing for next row.
Shape front slope
Dec 1 st at end of next and foll 6th row.
43 [45: 48: 50: 53] sts.
Work 5 rows, ending with RS facing for next row.
Shape raglan armhole
Cast off 2 sts at beg and dec 1 st at end of next row.
40 [42: 45: 47: 50] sts.
Work 1 row.
Working all raglan decreases as set by back, dec 1 st at raglan armhole edge of next 1 [1: 1: 1: 3] rows, then on 5 [4: 2: 1: 0] foll 4th rows, then on 23 [25: 30: 32: 34] foll alt rows **and at same time** dec 1 st at front slope edge on 5th and 4 [8: 7: 10: 10] foll 6th rows, then on every foll 8th [8th: 8th: 0: 0] row. 2 sts.
Work 1 row, ending with RS facing for next row.
Next row (RS): K2tog and fasten off.

RIGHT FRONT

Using 4mm (US 6) needles cast on 53 [55: 58: 60: 63] sts.

Work in g st for 8 rows, ending with RS facing for next row.
Change to 4½mm (US 7) needles.
Beg with a K row, work in st st for 12 rows, ending with RS facing for next row.
Next row (dec) (RS): K to last 24 [24: 26: 26: 28] sts, (sl 1, K1, psso, K10 [10: 11: 11: 12]) twice.
Complete to match left front, reversing shapings, working an extra row before beg of raglan armhole shaping.

SLEEVES

Using 4mm (US 6) needles cast on 59 [59: 61: 61: 63] sts.
Work in g st for 16 rows, ending with RS facing for next row.
Change to 4½mm (US 7) needles.
Beg with a K row, cont in st st, shaping sides by inc 1 st at each end of next and foll 18th row, then on every foll 20th row until there are 69 [69: 71: 71: 73] sts.
Cont straight until sleeve meas 44 [44: 45: 45: 45] cm, ending with RS facing for next row.
Shape raglan
Cast off 2 sts at beg of next 2 rows.
65 [65: 67: 67: 69] sts.
Working all raglan decreases as set by back, dec 1 st at each end of next and every foll 4th row to 55 [55: 57: 57: 59] sts, then on every foll alt row until 5 sts rem.
Work 1 row, ending with RS facing for next row.
Cast off rem 5 sts.

MAKING UP

Press as described on the information page.
Join raglan seams using back stitch, or mattress stitch if preferred.
Front bands (both alike)
With RS facing and using 4mm (US 6) needles, pick up and knit 58 [60: 60: 62: 62] sts along front opening edge, between cast-on edge and beg of front slope shaping.
Work in g st for 4 rows, ending with **WS** facing for next row.
Cast off knitwise (on **WS**).
Scarf collar (make 2)
Using 4½mm (US 7) needles cast on 48 sts.
Beg with a K row, work in st st for 18 rows, ending

with RS facing for next row.

Next row (RS): K2, M1, K to last 2 sts, M1, K2.
Working all increases as set by last row, inc 1 st
at each end of 18th and every foll 16th row until
there are 72 sts.

Cont straight until scarf meas 84 cm, ending with
RS facing for next row.

Change to 4mm (US 6) needles.

Work in g st for 5 rows, ending with **WS** facing for
next row.

Work fringe cast-off as folls: using double-
pointed needles, K2, *(without turning slip these
2 sts to opposite end of needle and bring yarn to
opposite end of work pulling it quite tightly
across WS of work, K these 2 sts again) 62 times,
K2tog and fasten off, K next 2 sts, rep from * until
all sts are cast off.

Knot ends of fringe. Join cast-on (centre back)

seam of scarf collar pieces, then sew one edge to
neck and front slope edges, beg and ending at

cast-off edges of front bands.

See information page for finishing instructions.

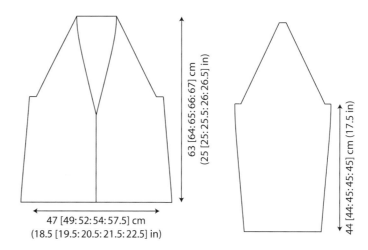

47 [49: 52: 54: 57.5] cm
(18.5 [19.5: 20.5: 21.5: 22.5] in)

63 [64: 65: 66: 67] cm
(25 [25: 25.5: 26: 26.5] in)

44 [44: 45: 45: 45] cm (17.5 in)

YARN

	XS	S	M	L	XL	
To fit bust	81	86	91	97	102	cm
	32	34	36	38	40	in

RYC Cashsoft Aran

| | 9 | 9 | 10 | 10 | 11 | x 50gm |

(photographed in Tornado 008)

NEEDLES

1 pair 4mm (no 8) (US 6) needles
1 pair 4½mm (no 7) (US 7) needles
4mm (no 8) (US 6) circular needle
Cable needle

ZIP – Open-ended zip to fit

TENSION

19 sts and 25 rows to 10 cm measured over
stocking stitch using 4½mm (US 7) needles.

SPECIAL ABBREVIATION

C6B = slip next 3 sts onto cable needle and leave
at back of work, K3, then K3 from cable needle.

BACK

Using 4mm (US 6) needles cast on 73 [77: 83:
87: 93] sts.
Row 1 (RS): K0 [1: 0: 0: 0], P2 [3: 1: 3: 0], *K3, P3,
rep from * to last 5 [1: 4: 0: 3] sts, K3 [1: 3: 0: 3],
P2 [0: 1: 0: 0].
Row 2: P0 [1: 0: 0: 0], K2 [3: 1: 3: 0], *P3, K3,
rep from * to last 5 [1: 4: 0: 3] sts, P3 [1: 3: 0: 3],
K2 [0: 1: 0: 0].
These 2 rows form rib.
Cont in rib for a further 19 rows, ending with **WS**
facing for next row.
Row 22 (WS): Rib 6 [8: 11: 13: 16], *(M1, rib 1)
twice, M1, rib 8, rep from * 5 times more, (M1, rib
1) twice, M1, rib to end. 94 [98: 104: 108: 114] sts.
Change to 4½mm (US 7) needles.
Row 1 (RS): P1 [1: 0: 0: 1], (K1, P1) 2 [3: 5: 6: 7]
times, *K6, (P1, K1) 3 times, P1, rep from * 5 times
more, K6, (P1, K1) 2 [3: 5: 6: 7] times, P1 [1: 0: 0: 1].
Row 2 and every foll alt row: P1 [1: 0: 0: 1], (K1,
P1) 2 [3: 5: 6: 7] times, *P6, (P1, K1) 3 times, P1,
rep from * 5 times more, P6, (P1, K1) 2 [3: 5:
6: 7] times, P1 [1: 0: 0: 1].
Row 3: P1 [1: 0: 0: 1], (K1, P1) 2 [3: 5: 6: 7] times,

*C6B, (P1, K1) 3 times, P1, rep from * 5 times more,
C6B, (P1, K1) 2 [3: 5: 6: 7] times, P1 [1: 0: 0: 1].
Row 5: As row 1.
Row 6: As row 2.
These 6 rows form patt.
Cont in patt, inc 1 st at each end of 5th and every
foll 10th row until there are 104 [108: 114:
118: 124] sts, taking inc sts into moss st.
Cont straight until back meas 33 [34: 34:
35: 35] cm, ending with RS facing for next row.
Shape armholes
Keeping patt correct, cast off 6 [7: 7: 8: 8] sts at
beg of next 2 rows. 92 [94: 100: 102: 108] sts.
Dec 1 st at each end of next 7 [7: 9: 9: 11] rows,
then on foll 6 alt rows.
66 [68: 70: 72: 74] sts.
Cont straight until armhole meas 20 [20: 21:
21: 22] cm, ending with RS facing for next row.
Shape shoulders and back neck
Cast off 5 [5: 6: 6: 6] sts at beg of next 2 rows.
56 [58: 58: 60: 62] sts.
Next row (RS): Cast off 5 [5: 6: 6: 6] sts, patt until
there are 10 [10: 9: 9: 10] sts on right needle and
turn, leaving rem sts on a holder.
Work each side of neck separately.
Cast off 4 sts at beg of next row.
Cast off rem 6 [6: 5: 5: 6] sts.
With RS facing, rejoin yarn to rem sts, cast off
centre 26 [28: 28: 30: 30] sts, patt to end.
Complete to match first side, reversing shapings.

LEFT FRONT

Using 4mm (US 6) needles cast on 37 [39: 42:
44: 47] sts.
Row 1 (RS): K0 [1: 0: 0: 0], P2 [3: 1: 3: 0], *K3, P3,
rep from * to last 5 sts, K5.
Row 2: K2, *P3, K3, rep from * to last 5 [1: 4: 0: 3]
sts, P3 [1: 3: 0: 3], K2 [0: 1: 0: 0].
These 2 rows form rib.
Cont in rib for a further 19 rows, ending with **WS**
facing for next row.
Row 22 (WS): Rib 10, *(M1, rib 1) twice, M1, rib 8,
rep from * once more, (M1, rib 1) twice, M1, rib to
end. 46 [48: 51: 53: 56] sts.
Change to 4½mm (US 7) needles.
Row 1 (RS): P1 [1: 0: 0: 1], (K1, P1) 2 [3: 5: 6: 7]
times, *K6, (P1, K1) 3 times, P1, rep from * twice
more, K2.

Row 2 and every foll alt row: K2, *P1, (K1, P1)
3 times, P6, rep from * twice more, (P1, K1) 2 [3: 5:
6: 7] times, P1 [1: 0: 0: 1].
Row 3: P1 [1: 0: 0: 1], (K1, P1) 2 [3: 5: 6: 7] times,
*C6B, (P1, K1) 3 times, P1, rep from * twice more,
K2.
Row 5: As row 1.
Row 6: As row 2.
These 6 rows form patt.
Cont in patt, inc 1 st at beg of 5th and every foll
10th row until there are 51 [53: 56: 58: 61] sts,
taking inc sts into moss st.
Cont straight until left front matches back to beg
of armhole shaping, ending with RS facing for
next row.
Shape armhole
Keeping patt correct, cast off 6 [7: 7: 8: 8] sts at
beg of next row.
45 [46: 49: 50: 53] sts.
Work 1 row.
Dec 1 st at armhole edge of next 7 [7: 9: 9: 11] rows,
then on foll 6 alt rows. 32 [33: 34: 35: 36] sts.
Cont straight until 15 [15: 15: 17: 17] rows less
have been worked than on back to beg of shoulder
shaping, ending with **WS** facing for next row.
Shape neck
Keeping patt correct, cast off 7 [8: 8: 8: 8] sts at
beg of next row.
25 [25: 26: 27: 28] sts.
Dec 1 st at neck edge of next 6 rows, then on foll
2 [2: 2: 3: 3] alt rows, then on foll 4th row, ending
with RS facing for next row. 16 [16: 17: 17: 18] sts.
Shape shoulder
Cast off 5 [5: 6: 6: 6] sts at beg of next and foll alt
row.
Work 1 row.
Cast off rem 6 [6: 5: 5: 6] sts.

RIGHT FRONT

Using 4mm (US 6) needles cast on 37 [39: 42:
44: 47] sts.
Row 1 (RS): K2, *K3, P3, rep from * to last 5 [1: 4:
0: 3] sts, K3 [1: 3: 0: 3], P2 [0: 1: 0: 0].
Row 2: P0 [1: 0: 0: 0], K2 [3: 1: 3: 0], *P3, K3,
rep from * to last 5 sts, P3, K2.
These 2 rows form rib.
Cont in rib for a further 19 rows, ending with **WS**
facing for next row.

Row 22 (WS): Rib 6 [8: 11: 13: 16], *(M1, rib 1) twice, M1, rib 8, rep from * twice more, rib 1.
46 [48: 51: 53: 56] sts.
Change to 4½mm (US 7) needles.
Row 1 (RS): K2, *P1, (K1, P1) 3 times, K6, rep from * twice more, (P1, K1) 2 [3: 5: 6: 7] times, P1 [1: 0: 0: 1].
Row 2 and every foll alt row: P1 [1: 0: 0: 1], (K1, P1) 2 [3: 5: 6: 7] times, *P6, (P1, K1) 3 times, P1, rep from * twice more, K2.
Row 3: K2, *P1, (K1, P1) 3 times, C6B, rep from * twice more, (P1, K1) 2 [3: 5: 6: 7] times, P1 [1: 0: 0: 1].
Row 5: As row 1.
Row 6: As row 2.
These 6 rows form patt.
Cont in patt, inc 1 st at end of 5th and every foll 10th row until there are 51 [53: 56: 58: 61] sts, taking inc sts into moss st.
Complete to match left front, reversing shapings, working an extra row before beg of armhole, neck and shoulder shaping.

MAKING UP
Press as described on the information page.
Join shoulder seams using back stitch, or mattress stitch if preferred.
Collar
With RS facing and using 4mm (US 6) circular needle, beg and ending at front opening edges, pick up and knit 24 [26: 26: 28: 28] sts up right side of neck, 25 [27: 27: 29: 29] sts from back, then 24 [26: 26: 28: 28] sts down left side of neck. 73 [79: 79: 85: 85] sts.
Row 1 (WS): K5, *P3, K3, rep from * to last 2 sts, K2.
Row 2: K2, *P3, K3, rep from * to last 5 sts, P3, K2.
Rep last 2 rows until collar meas 16 cm.
Cast off in rib.
Armhole borders (both alike)
With RS facing and using 4mm (US 6) needles, pick up and knit 87 [87: 93: 93: 99] sts evenly all round armhole edge.
Row 1 (WS): K3, *P3, K3, rep from * to end.
Row 2: P3, *K3, P3, rep from * to end.

Rep last 2 rows twice more, then row 1 again, ending with RS facing for next row.
Cast off in rib.
See information page for finishing instructions.
Insert zip into front opening, positioning top of zip 7 cm above collar pick-up row. Fold collar in half to inside and slip st in place.

53 [54: 55: 56: 57] cm
(21 [21.5: 21.5: 22: 22.5] in)

43.5 [46: 49: 51: 54] cm
(17 [18: 19.5: 20: 21.5] in)

Nessie

YARN

	XS	S	M	L	XL
To fit bust	81	86	91	97	102 cm
	32	34	36	38	40 in

RYC Cashsoft Aran

	7	7	7	8	8	x 50gm

(photographed in Mole 003)

NEEDLES

1 pair 4mm (no 8) (US 6) needles
1 pair 4½mm (no 7) (US 7) needles
4mm (no 8) (US 6) circular needle

TENSION

19 sts and 25 rows to 10 cm measured over
stocking stitch using 4½mm (US 7) needles.

BACK

Using 4mm (US 6) needles cast on 74 [78: 86:
90: 94] sts.
Row 1 (RS): K2, *P2, K2, rep from * to end.
Row 2: P2, *K2, P2, rep from * to end.
These 2 rows form rib.
Cont in rib for a further 20 rows, inc [inc: dec:
dec: inc] 1 st at end of last row and ending with
RS facing for next row. 75 [79: 85: 89: 95] sts.
Change to 4½mm (US 7) needles.
Beg with a K row, cont in st st, inc 1 st at each
end of 13th and every foll 12th row until there are
83 [87: 93: 97: 103] sts.
Cont straight until back meas 33 [34: 34:
35: 35] cm, ending with RS facing for next row.
Shape armholes
Cast off 5 [6: 6: 7: 7] sts at beg of next 2 rows.
73 [75: 81: 83: 89] sts.
Dec 1 st at each end of next 7 [7: 9: 9: 11] rows,
then on foll 6 alt rows. 47 [49: 51: 53: 55] sts.
Cont straight until armhole meas 20 [20: 21:
21: 22] cm, ending with RS facing for next row.
Shape shoulders and back neck
Next row (RS): Cast off 5 [5: 6: 6: 6] sts, K until
there are 10 [10: 10: 10: 11] sts on right needle
and turn, leaving rem sts on a holder.
Work each side of neck separately.
Cast off 4 sts at beg of next row.
Cast off rem 6 [6: 6: 6: 7] sts.
With RS facing, rejoin yarn to rem sts, cast off

centre 17 [19: 19: 21: 21] sts, K to end.
Complete to match first side, reversing shapings.

FRONT

Work as given for back until 12 rows less have
been worked than on back to beg of armhole
shaping, ending with RS facing for next row.
Divide for neck
Next row (RS): K41 [43: 46: 48: 51] and turn,
leaving rem sts on a holder.
Work each side of neck separately.
Work 3 rows.
Next row (RS): K to last 4 sts, sl 1, K1, psso, K2.
Working all neck decreases as set by last row,
dec 1 st at neck edge on foll 4th row.
39 [41: 44: 46: 49] sts.
Work 3 rows, ending with RS facing for next row.
Shape armhole
Cast off 5 [6: 6: 7: 7] sts at beg and dec 1 st at
end of next row. 33 [34: 37: 38: 41] sts.
Work 1 row.
Dec 1 st at armhole edge of next 7 [7: 9: 9: 11]
rows, then on foll 6 alt rows **and at same time**
dec 1 st at neck edge on 3rd and every foll 4th
row. 15 [16: 17: 18: 18] sts.
Dec 1 st at neck edge **only** on 4th [4th: 2nd: 2nd:
4th] and every foll 6th [4th: 4th: 4th: 4th] row to
11 [12: 14: 12: 15] sts, then on every foll – [6th: 6th:
-: 6th] row until - [11: 12: -: 13] sts rem.
Cont straight until front matches back to beg of
shoulder shaping, ending with RS facing for next
row.
Shape shoulder
Cast off 5 [5: 6: 6: 6] sts at beg of next row.
Work 1 row.
Cast off rem 6 [6: 6: 6: 7] sts.
With RS facing, slip centre st onto a holder, rejoin
yarn to rem sts, K to end.
Work 3 rows.
Next row (RS): K2, K2tog, K to end.
Working all neck decreases as set by last row,
complete to match first side, reversing shapings,
working an extra row before beg of armhole and
shoulder shaping.

MAKING UP

Press as described on the information page.

Join shoulder seams using back stitch, or
mattress stitch if preferred.
Neckband
With RS facing and using 4mm (US 6) circular
needle, beg and ending at left shoulder seam,
pick up and knit 50 [50: 54: 54: 58] sts down left
side of neck, K st from front holder and mark this
st with a coloured thread, pick up and knit
50 [50: 54: 54: 58] sts up right side of neck, then
26 [26: 26: 30: 30] sts from back.
127 [127: 135: 139: 147] sts.
Round 1 (RS): *K2, P2, rep from * to within 2 sts
of marked st, K2tog tbl, K marked st, K2tog, P2,
**K2, P2, rep from ** to end.
This round sets position of rib.
Keeping rib correct, cont as folls:
Round 2: Rib to marked st, K marked st, rib to
end.
Round 3: Rib to within 2 sts of marked st,
work2tog tbl, K marked st, work2tog, rib to end.
Rep last 2 rounds 5 times more, then round 2
again. 113 [113: 121: 125: 133] sts.
Cast off in rib, still decreasing either side of
marked st as before.
Armhole borders (both alike)
With RS facing and using 4mm (US 6) needles,
pick up and knit 82 [86: 90: 94: 98] sts evenly all
round armhole edge.
Work in rib as given for back for 7 rows, ending
with RS facing for next row.
Cast off in rib.
See information page for finishing instructions.

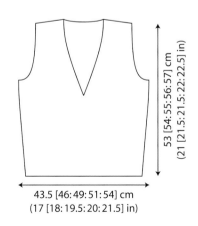

53 [54: 55: 56: 57] cm
(21 [21.5: 21.5: 22: 22.5] in)

43.5 [46: 49: 51: 54] cm
(17 [18: 19.5: 20: 21.5] in)

Skye

YARN

	XS	S	M	L	XL	
To fit bust	81	86	91	97	102	cm
	32	34	36	38	40	in
RYC Cashsoft Aran						
A Mole 003	11	11	12	12	13	x 50gm
B Oat 001	6	6	7	7	7	x 50gm

NEEDLES

1 pair 4mm (no 8) (US 6) needles
1 pair 4½mm (no 7) (US 7) needles
4mm (no 8) (US 6) circular needle

BUTTONS – 8 x 00317

TENSION

21 sts and 24 rows to 10 cm measured over patterned stocking stitch using 4½mm (US 7) needles.

BACK

Using 4mm (US 6) needles and yarn A cast on 105 [111: 117: 123: 129] sts.
Row 1 (RS): K0 [3: 0: 3: 0], *P3, K3, rep from * to last 3 [0: 3: 0: 3] sts, P3 [0: 3: 0: 3].
Row 2: P0 [3: 0: 3: 0], *K3, P3, rep from * to last 3 [0: 3: 0: 3] sts, K3 [0: 3: 0: 3].
These 2 rows form rib.
Cont in rib for a further 20 rows, ending with RS facing for next row.

Change to 4½mm (US 7) needles.
Beg and ending rows as indicated, using the **fairisle** technique as described on the information page and repeating the 26 row patt repeat throughout, cont in patt from chart for body, which is worked entirely in st st, as folls:
Dec 1 st at each end of 9th and every foll 8th row to 99 [105: 111: 117: 123] sts, then on foll 6th row, then on every foll 4th row until 85 [91: 97: 103: 109] sts rem.
Cont straight until back meas 34 [35: 35: 36: 36] cm, ending with RS facing for next row.
Inc 1 st at each end of next and foll 6th row, then on every foll 8th row until there are 95 [101: 107: 113: 119] sts, taking inc sts into patt.
Work 7 rows, ending with RS facing for next row.
(Back should meas 50 [51: 51: 52: 52] cm.)
Shape armholes
Keeping patt correct, cast off 5 [6: 6: 7: 7] sts at beg of next 2 rows. 85 [89: 95: 99: 105] sts.
Dec 1 st at each end of next 5 [5: 7: 7: 9] rows, then on foll 2 [3: 3: 4: 4] alt rows, then on foll 4th row. 69 [71: 73: 75: 77] sts.
Cont straight until armhole meas 22 [22: 23: 23: 24] cm, ending with RS facing for next row.
Shape shoulders and back neck
Cast off 7 [7: 7: 7: 8] sts at beg of next 2 rows. 55 [57: 59: 61: 61] sts.
Next row (RS): Cast off 7 [7: 7: 7: 8] sts, patt until there are 11 [11: 12: 12: 11] sts on right needle and

turn, leaving rem sts on a holder.
Work each side of neck separately.
Cast off 4 sts at beg of next row.
Cast off rem 7 [7: 8: 8: 7] sts.
With RS facing, rejoin yarns to rem sts, cast off centre 19 [21: 21: 23: 23] sts, patt to end.
Complete to match first side, reversing shapings.

LEFT FRONT

Using 4mm (US 6) needles and yarn A cast on 53 [56: 59: 62: 65] sts.
Row 1 (RS): K0 [3: 0: 3: 0], *P3, K3, rep from * to last 5 sts, P3, K2.
Row 2: P2, *K3, P3, rep from * to last 3 [0: 3: 0: 3] sts, K3 [0: 3: 0: 3].
These 2 rows form rib.
Cont in rib for a further 20 rows, ending with RS facing for next row.
Change to 4½mm (US 7) needles.
Beg and ending rows as indicated, cont in patt from chart for body as folls:
Dec 1 st at beg of 9th and every foll 8th row to 50 [53: 56: 59: 62] sts, then on foll 6th row, then on every foll 4th row until 43 [46: 49: 52: 55] sts rem.
Cont straight until left front meas 34 [35: 35: 36: 36] cm, ending with RS facing for next row.
Inc 1 st at beg of next and foll 6th row, then on every foll 8th row until there are 47 [50: 53: 56: 59] sts, taking inc sts into patt.

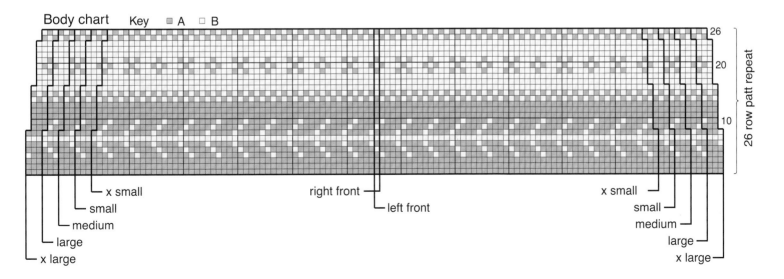

Body chart   Key ■ A □ B

26   20   10   26 row patt repeat

x small
small
medium
large
x large

right front
left front

x small
small
medium
large
x large

Work 3 rows, ending with RS facing for next row.

Shape front slope

Keeping patt correct, dec 1 st at end of next and 2 foll 4th rows **and at same time** inc 1 st at beg of 5th row. 45 [48: 51: 54: 57] sts.

Work 3 rows, ending with RS facing for next row. (Left front should now match back to beg of armhole shaping.)

Shape armhole

Keeping patt correct, cast off 5 [6: 6: 7: 7] sts at beg and dec 1 st at end of next row.

39 [41: 44: 46: 49] sts.

Work 1 row.

Dec 1 st at armhole edge of next 5 [5: 7: 7: 9] rows, then on foll 2 [3: 3: 4: 4] alt rows, then on foll 4th row **and at same time** dec 1 st at front slope edge on 3rd and every foll 4th row.

28 [28: 29: 29: 30] sts.

Dec 1 st at front slope edge **only** on 2nd [4th: 2nd: 4th: 2nd] and every foll 4th row to 23 [21: 24: 22: 24] sts, then on every foll 6th [-: 6th: -: 6th] row until 21 [-: 22: -: 23] sts rem.

Cont straight until left front matches back to beg of shoulder shaping, ending with RS facing for next row.

Shape shoulder

Cast off 7 [7: 7: 7: 8] sts at beg of next and foll alt row.

Work 1 row.

Cast off rem 7 [7: 8: 8: 7] sts.

RIGHT FRONT

Using 4mm (US 6) needles and yarn A cast on 53 [56: 59: 62: 65] sts.

Row 1 (RS): K2, *P3, K3, rep from * to last 3 [0: 3: 0: 3] sts, P3 [0: 3: 0: 3].

Row 2: P0 [3: 0: 3: 0], *K3, P3, rep from * to last 5 sts, K3, P2.

These 2 rows form rib.

Cont in rib for a further 20 rows, ending with RS facing for next row.

Change to 4½mm (US 7) needles.

Beg and ending rows as indicated, cont in patt from chart for body as folls:

Dec 1 st at end of 9th and every foll 8th row to 50 [53: 56: 59: 62] sts, then on foll 6th row, then on every foll 4th row until 43 [46: 49: 52: 55] sts rem.

Complete to match left front, reversing shapings, working an extra row before beg of armhole and shoulder shaping.

SLEEVES

Using 4mm (US 6) needles and yarn A cast on 51 [51: 53: 55: 55] sts.

Row 1 (RS): P0 [0: 1: 2: 2], K3, *P3, K3, rep from * to last 0 [0: 1: 2: 2] sts, P0 [0: 1: 2: 2].

Row 2: K0 [0: 1: 2: 2], P3, *K3, P3, rep from * to last 0 [0: 1: 2: 2] sts, K0 [0: 1: 2: 2].

These 2 rows form rib.

Cont in rib for a further 20 rows, ending with RS facing for next row.

Change to 4½mm (US 7) needles.

Beg and ending rows as indicated, cont in patt from chart for sleeve, shaping sides by inc 1 st at each end of next and every foll 8th [6th: 6th: 8th: 6th] row to 67 [55: 57: 77: 65] sts, then on every foll 10th [8th: 8th: -: 8th] row until there are 71 [73: 75: -: 79] sts, taking inc sts into patt.

Cont straight until sleeve meas approx 44 [45: 45: 46: 46] cm, ending after same chart row as on back to beg of armhole shaping and with RS facing for next row.

Shape top

Keeping patt correct, cast off 5 [6: 6: 7: 7] sts at beg of next 2 rows. 61 [61: 63: 63: 65] sts.

Dec 1 st at each end of next 5 rows, then on foll 3 alt rows, then on every foll 4th row until 41 [41: 43: 43: 45] sts rem.

Work 1 row, ending with RS facing for next row.

Dec 1 st at each end of next and every foll alt row to 31 sts, then on foll 5 rows, ending with RS facing for next row.

Cast off rem 21 sts.

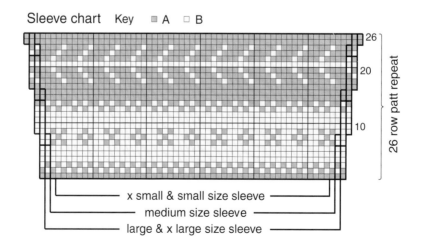

Sleeve chart   Key   ▦ A   ☐ B

26 row patt repeat

— x small & small size sleeve —
— medium size sleeve —
— large & x large size sleeve —

MAKING UP

Press as described on the information page. Join shoulder seams using back stitch, or mattress stitch if preferred.

Front band

With RS facing, using 4mm (US 6) circular needle and yarn A, beg and ending at cast-on edges, pick up and knit 86 [88: 88: 90: 90] sts up right front opening edge to beg of front slope shaping, 59 [59: 62: 62: 65] sts up right front slope to shoulder, 27 [29: 29: 31: 31] sts from back, 59 [59: 62: 62: 65] sts down left front slope to beg of front slope shaping, then 86 [88: 88: 90: 90] sts down left front opening edge. 317 [323: 329: 335: 341] sts.

Row 1 (WS): K1, P3, *K3, P3, rep from * to last st, K1.

Row 2: K4, *P3, K3, rep from * to last st, K1. These 2 rows form rib.

Work in rib for 1 row more, ending with RS facing for next row.

Row 4 (RS): Rib 4 [2: 2: 2: 2], *work 2 tog, yrn (to make a buttonhole), rib 9 [10: 10: 10: 10], rep from * 6 times more, work 2 tog, yrn (to make 8th buttonhole), rib to end.

Work in rib for a further 3 rows, ending with RS facing for next row.
Cast off in rib.

Belt

Using 4mm (US 6) needles and yarn A cast on 23 sts.

Row 1 (RS): sl 1 knitwise, (K3, P3) 3 times, K4.

Row 2: sl 1 purlwise, (P3, K3) 3 times, P3, K1.

Rep these 2 rows until belt meas 150 cm.
Cast off in rib.

See information page for finishing instructions, setting in sleeves using the set-in method.

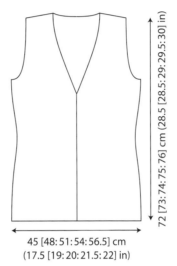

72 [73: 74: 75: 76] cm (28.5 [28.5: 29: 29.5: 30] in)

45 [48: 51: 54: 56.5] cm
(17.5 [19: 20: 21.5: 22] in)

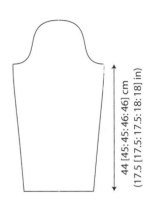

44 [45: 45: 46: 46] cm
(17.5 [17.5: 17.5: 18: 18] in)

Katrine

YARN

	XS	S	M	L	XL
To fit bust	81	86	91	97	102 cm
	32	34	36	38	40 in

RYC Cashsoft Aran

| | 11 | 11 | 12 | 12 | 13 x 50gm |

(photographed in Bud 006)

NEEDLES

1 pair 4mm (no 8) (US 6) needles
1 pair 4½mm (no 7) (US 7) needles

ZIP – 10 cm zip

TENSION

19 sts and 25 rows to 10 cm measured over
stocking stitch using 4½mm (US 7) needles.

BACK

Using 4mm (US 6) needles cast on 74 [78: 86:
90: 94] sts.
Row 1 (RS): K2, *P2, K2, rep from * to end.
Row 2: P2, *K2, P2, rep from * to end.
These 2 rows form rib.
Work in rib for a further 26 rows, inc [inc: dec:
dec: inc] 1 st at end of last row and ending with
RS facing for next row.
75 [79: 85: 89: 95] sts.
Change to 4½mm (US 7) needles.
Beg with a K row, work in st st, shaping side
seams by inc 1 st at each end of 7th and every foll
8th row until there are 85 [89: 95: 99: 105] sts.
Cont straight until back meas 28 [29: 29:
30: 30] cm, ending with RS facing for next row.
Shape raglan armholes
Cast off 4 sts at beg of next 2 rows.
77 [81: 87: 91: 97] sts.
XS and S only
Next row (RS): K2, sl 1, K1, psso, K to last 4 sts,
K2tog, K2.
Next row: K2, P to last 2 sts, K2.
Next row: Knit.
Next row: K2, P to last 2 sts, K2.

Rep last 4 rows 1 [0: -: -: -] times more.
73 [79: -: -: -] sts.
M, L and XL only
Next row (RS): K2, sl 1, K1, psso, K to last 4 sts,
K2tog, K2.
Next row: K2, P2tog, P to last 5 sts, P2tog tbl, K2.
Rep last 2 rows – [-: 0: 1: 3] times more.
- [-: 83: 83: 81] sts.
All sizes
Next row (RS): K2, sl 1, K1, psso, K to last 4 sts,
K2tog, K2.
Next row: K2, P to last 2 sts, K2.
Rep last 2 rows 23 [25: 27: 26: 25] times more.
25 [27: 27: 29: 29] sts.
Shape back neck
Next row (RS): K2, sl 1, K1, psso and turn, leaving
rem sts on a holder.
Work each side of neck separately.
Dec 1 st at neck edge of next row.
Next row (RS): K2tog and fasten off.
With RS facing, rejoin yarn to rem sts, cast off
centre 18 [20: 20: 22: 22] sts, K to end.
Complete to match first side, reversing shapings.

FRONT

Work as given for back until 63 [65: 65: 69: 69] sts
rem in raglan armhole shaping.
Work 1 row, ending with RS facing for next row.
Divide for front opening
Next row (RS): K2, sl 1, K1, psso, K27 [28: 28:
30: 30] and turn, leaving rem sts on a holder.
Work each side of neck separately.
Dec 1 st at raglan armhole edge of 2nd and foll
12 alt rows, ending with **WS** facing for next row.
17 [18: 18: 20: 20] sts.
Shape neck
Cast off 5 [6: 6: 6: 6] sts at beg of next row.
12 [12: 12: 14: 14] sts.
Dec 1 st at neck edge of next 5 rows, then on foll
0 [0: 0: 1: 1] alt row **and at same time** dec 1 st at
raglan armhole edge of next and every foll alt
row. 4 sts.
Work 1 row, ending with RS facing for next row.

Next row (RS): K1, sl 1, K2tog, psso.
2 sts.
Next row: K2.
Next row: K2tog and fasten off.
With RS facing, rejoin yarn to rem sts, K2tog, K to
last 4 sts, K2tog, K2.
Complete to match first side, reversing shapings.

SLEEVES

Using 4mm (US 6) needles cast on 46 [46: 46:
50: 50] sts.
Work in rib as given for back for 28 rows, ending
with RS facing for next row.
Change to 4½mm (US 7) needles.
Beg with a K row, cont in st st, shaping sides by
inc 1 st at each end of next and every foll
6th [6th: 6th: 8th: 6th] row to 52 [52: 58:
64: 54] sts, then on every foll 8th [8th: 8th: 10th:
8th] row until there are 68 [68: 70: 70: 72] sts.
Cont straight until sleeve meas 45 [45: 46:
46: 46] cm, ending with RS facing for next row.
Shape raglan
Cast off 4 sts at beg of next 2 rows.
60 [60: 62: 62: 64] sts.
Working all raglan decreases as set by back, dec
1 st at each end of next and every foll 4th row to
54 [54: 56: 56: 58] sts, then on every foll alt row
until 10 sts rem.
Work 1 row, ending with RS facing for next row.
Left sleeve only
Dec 1 st at each end of next row, then cast off
2 sts at beg of foll row. 6 sts.
Dec 1 st at beg of next row, then cast off 3 sts at
beg of foll row.
Right sleeve only
Cast off 3 sts at beg and dec 1 st at end of next
row. 6 sts.
Work 1 row.
Cast off 4 sts at beg of next row.
Work 1 row.
Both sleeves
Next row (RS): K2tog and fasten off.

MAKING UP

Press as described on the information page.
Join raglan seams using back stitch, or mattress stitch if preferred.

Collar

With RS facing and using 4mm (US 6) needles, beg and ending at front opening edges, pick up and knit 14 [15: 15: 17: 17] sts up right side of neck, 6 sts from right sleeve, 22 [24: 24: 26: 26] sts from back, 6 sts from left sleeve, then 14 [15: 15: 17: 17] sts down left side of neck.
62 [66: 66: 72: 72] sts.

Row 1 (RS of collar, WS of body): P3 [5: 5: 10: 6], inc in next st, *P1, inc in next st, rep from * to last 4 [6: 6: 11: 7] sts, P to end. 90 [94: 94: 98: 102] sts.
Beg with row 2, work in rib as given for back for 7 cm, ending with **WS** of collar facing for next row.

Next row (WS of collar): P2, *K1, M1, K1, P2, rep from * to end. 112 [117: 117: 122: 127] sts.
Change to 4½mm (US 7) needles.

Next row: K2, *P3, K2, rep from * to end.
Next row: P2, *K3, P2, rep from * to end.
Rep last 2 rows until collar meas 31 cm.

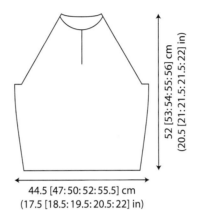

52 [53: 54: 55: 56] cm
(20.5 [21: 21.5: 21.5: 22] in)

44.5 [47: 50: 52: 55.5] cm
(17.5 [18.5: 19.5: 20.5: 22] in)

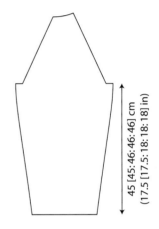

45 [45: 46: 46: 46] cm
(17.5 [17.5: 18: 18: 18] in)

Cast off in rib.
See information page for finishing instructions.
Insert zip into front opening.

Bonnie blanket

YARN

RYC Cashsoft Aran

A Oat	001	5	x 50gm
B Foxglove	002	5	x 50gm
C Mole	003	5	x 50gm
D Haze	004	5	x 50gm
E Burst	005	5	x 50gm
F Bud	006	5	x 50gm
G Kale	007	5	x 50gm
H Tornado	008	5	x 50gm

NEEDLES

1 pair 4½mm (no 7) (US 7) needles

FINISHED SIZE

Completed blanket measures 126 cm (49½in) by 168 cm (66 ins).

TENSION

Based on a stocking stitch tension of 19 sts and 25 rows to 10 cm using 4½mm (US 7) needles. Basic motif measures 14 cm square.

BASIC MOTIF

Using 4½mm (US 7) needles and first colour cast on 89 sts.

Row 1 (WS): Using first colour, knit.

Row 2: Using first colour, K2tog, (K19, K3tog) 3 times, K19, K2tog. 81 sts.

Row 3 and every foll alt row: Knit to end, using same colour as used for previous row.

Row 4: Using first colour, K2tog, (K17, K3tog) 3 times, K17, K2tog. 73 sts.
Join in second colour.

Row 6: Using second colour, K2tog, (K15, K3tog) 3 times, K15, K2tog. 65 sts.

Row 8: Using second colour, K2tog, (K13, K3tog) 3 times, K13, K2tog. 57 sts.

Row 10: Using first colour, K2tog, (K11, K3tog) 3 times, K11, K2tog. 49 sts.

Row 12: Using first colour, K2tog, (K9, K3tog) 3 times, K9, K2tog. 41 sts.

Row 14: Using second colour, K2tog, (K7, K3tog) 3 times, K7, K2tog. 33 sts.

Row 16: Using second colour, K2tog, (K5, K3tog) 3 times, K5, K2tog. 25 sts.

Row 18: Using first colour, K2tog, (K3, K3tog) 3 times, K3, K2tog. 17 sts.

Row 20: Using first colour, K2tog, (K1, K3tog) 3 times, K1, K2tog. 9 sts.

Row 21: As row 3.

Row 22: Using first colour, (K3tog) 3 times. 3 sts.

Row 23: K3tog and fasten off.
Join row-end edges to form a square.

BLANKET

Following diagram, make and join 108 basic motifs to form a rectangle 9 motifs wide and 12 motifs long. Use colours as indicated on diagram – first letter indicates first colour, with second letter indicating second colour for this motif.
Press as described on the information page.

EB	CD	EG	AC	EH	DC	EF	AC	GD
DE	EB	BC	GD	FB	GA	FH	BG	AF
HA	DG	HG	AE	HF	CB	CD	DF	HE
BF	FE	CA	GF	DE	HD	DH	GA	CB
FA	DH	EF	BA	HB	CA	EC	BF	HG
BE	CE	BH	HC	FA	GH	CF	HA	DB
CF	BH	EH	FD	GB	BC	EH	AB	CG
AB	EA	FB	CE	DF	HE	AG	GD	BC
FH	AD	GB	AH	GB	AH	HC	AF	GE
DB	HG	FD	GC	AE	GC	FA	HE	AD
EA	DG	EC	BD	FG	DA	ED	BD	CH
AF	BE	HA	CG	AH	EG	FC	GF	BA

Bonnie scarf

YARN

RYC Cashsoft Aran

A Oat	001	2	x 50gm
B Foxglove	002	2	x 50gm
C Mole	003	2	x 50gm
D Haze	004	2	x 50gm
E Burst	005	2	x 50gm
F Bud	006	2	x 50gm
G Kale	007	2	x 50gm
H Tornado	008	2	x 50gm

NEEDLES

1 pair 4½mm (no 7) (US 7) needles

FINISHED SIZE

Completed scarf measures 28 cm (11 in) wide and 224 cm (88 ins) long.

TENSION

Based on a stocking stitch tension of 19 sts and 25 rows to 10 cm using 4½mm (US 7) needles. Basic motif measures 14 cm square.

SCARF

Following diagram, make and join 32 basic motifs as given for Bonnie blanket to form a strip 2 motifs wide and 16 motifs long. Use colours as indicated on diagram – first letter indicates first colour, with second letter indicating second colour for this motif.

Press as described on the information page.

HB	AG
ED	CB
FG	HD
AE	FB
CD	GA
EB	BG
DG	CF
HA	BE
BC	FH
DH	GB
EF	AH
DF	GD
CE	FA
DA	HC
EH	BF
AC	GE

 Bonnie bag

YARN

RYC Cashsoft Aran

A	Oat	001	1	x 50gm
B	Foxglove	002	1	x 50gm
C	Mole	003	1	x 50gm
D	Haze	004	1	x 50gm
E	Burst	005	1	x 50gm
F	Bud	006	1	x 50gm
G	Kale	007	1	x 50gm
H	Tornado	008	1	x 50gm

NEEDLES

1 pair 4½mm (no 7) (US 7) needles

EXTRAS – Piece of lining fabric 70 cm x 35 cm and matching thread

FINISHED SIZE

Completed bag measures 28 cm (11 in) square.

TENSION

Based on a stocking stitch tension of 19 sts and 25 rows to 10 cm using 4½mm (US 7) needles. Basic motif measures 14 cm square.

SIDES (make 2)

Following diagrams, make and join 8 basic motifs as given for Bonnie blanket to form 2 squares, each 2 motifs wide and 2 motifs long. Use colours as indicated on diagram – first letter indicates first colour, with second letter indicating second colour for this motif.

HANDLES (make 2)

First handle

Using 4½mm (US 7) needles and yarn B cast on 70 sts.
Work in g st for 9 rows, ending with **WS** facing for next row.
Cast off knitwise (on **WS**).

Second handle

Work as given for first handle but using yarn H.

MAKING UP

Press as described on the information page. From lining fabric, cut out pieces same size as sides, adding seam allowance along all edges. Join sides along 3 edges, leaving opening along upper edge. Sew ends of handle inside upper edge, positioning handles approx 4 cm in from side seams.
Join lining pieces in same way as for knitted side pieces. Fold seam allowance to WS around upper edge. Slip lining inside bag and slip st upper edge in place.

First side

BH	CE
AF	GD

Second side

GB	EA
FH	DC

 # Dundee

YARN

	XS	S	M	L	XL	
To fit bust	81	86	91	97	102	cm
	32	34	36	38	40	in

RYC Cashsoft Aran

	12	12	13	13	14	x 50gm

(photographed in Burst 005)

NEEDLES

1 pair 4mm (no 8) (US 6) needles
1 pair 4½mm (no 7) (US 7) needles
Cable needle

ZIP – Open-ended zip to fit

TENSION

19 sts and 25 rows to 10 cm measured over stocking stitch using 4½mm (US 7) needles.

SPECIAL ABBREVIATIONS

C4B = slip next 2 sts onto cable needle and leave at back of work, K2, then K2 from cable needle;
C4F = slip next 2 sts onto cable needle and leave at front of work, K2, then K2 from cable needle;
Cr3R = slip next st onto cable needle and leave at back of work, K2, then P1 from cable needle;
Cr3L = slip next 2 sts onto cable needle and leave at front of work, P1, then K2 from cable needle;

C5F = slip next 2 sts onto cable needle and leave at front of work, P1, K2, then K2 from cable needle.

BACK

Using 4mm (US 6) needles cast on 74 [78: 84: 88: 94] sts.
Row 1 (RS): K0 [0: 1: 0: 0], P2 [0: 2: 1: 0], *K2, P2, rep from * to last 0 [2: 1: 3: 2] sts, K0 [2: 1: 2: 2], P0 [0: 0: 1: 0].
Row 2: P0 [0: 1: 0: 0], K2 [0: 2: 1: 0], *P2, K2, rep from * to last 0 [2: 1: 3: 2] sts, P0 [2: 1: 2: 2], K0 [0: 0: 1: 0].
These 2 rows form rib.
Cont in rib for a further 19 rows, ending with **WS** facing for next row.
Row 22 (WS): Rib 11 [13: 16: 18: 21], *(M1, rib 2) 3 times, M1, rib 7, M1, rib 3, M1, rib 7, rep from * once more, (M1, rib 2) 3 times, M1, rib to end.
90 [94: 100: 104: 110] sts.
Change to 4½mm (US 7) needles.
Beg and ending rows as indicated and repeating the 24 row patt repeat throughout, cont in patt from chart for body as folls:
Inc 1 st at each end of 7th and every foll 8th row until there are 104 [108: 114: 118: 124] sts, taking inc sts into double moss st.
Cont straight until back meas 33 [34: 34:

35: 35] cm, ending with RS facing for next row.
Shape armholes
Keeping patt correct, cast off 5 [6: 6: 7: 7] sts at beg of next 2 rows. 94 [96: 102: 104: 110] sts.
Dec 1 st at each end of next 3 [3: 5: 5: 7] rows, then on foll 3 alt rows, then on every foll 4th row until 78 [80: 82: 84: 86] sts rem.
Cont straight until armhole meas 20 [20: 21: 21: 22] cm, ending with RS facing for next row.
Shape shoulders and back neck
Cast off 7 [7: 8: 8: 8] sts at beg of next 2 rows. 64 [66: 66: 68: 70] sts.
Next row (RS): Cast off 7 [7: 8: 8: 8] sts, patt until there are 12 [12: 11: 11: 12] sts on right needle and turn, leaving rem sts on a holder.
Work each side of neck separately.
Cast off 4 sts at beg of next row.
Cast off rem 8 [8: 7: 7: 8] sts.
With RS facing, rejoin yarn to rem sts, cast off centre 26 [28: 28: 30: 30] sts dec 6 sts evenly, patt to end.
Complete to match first side, reversing shapings.

LEFT FRONT

Using 4mm (US 6) needles cast on 38 [40: 43: 45: 48] sts.
Row 1 (RS): K0 [0: 1: 0: 0], P2 [0: 2: 1: 0], *K2, P2, rep from * to last 4 sts, K4.

Key

- ☐ K on RS, P on WS
- ▪ P on RS, K on WS
- ◉ { On Back: P on RS / On Front: K on RS }
- ▨ Cr3R
- ▧ Cr3L
- ◢ C4B
- ◢ C4F
- ◢ C5F

Body chart

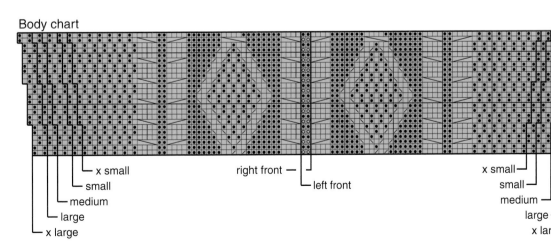

right front — left front

x small — small — medium — large — x large

x small — small — medium — large — x large

24 row patt repeat

24 20 10

Row 2: K2, *P2, K2, rep from * to last 0 [2: 1: 3: 2] sts, P0 [2: 1: 2: 2], K0 [0: 0: 1: 0].

These 2 rows form rib.

Cont in rib for a further 19 rows, ending with **WS** facing for next row.

Row 22 (WS): (Rib 2, M1) twice, rib 7, M1, rib 3, M1, rib 7, (M1, rib 2) 3 times, M1, rib to end. 46 [48: 51: 53: 56] sts.

Change to 4½mm (US 7) needles.

Beg and ending rows as indicated, cont in patt from chart for body as folls:

Inc 1 st at beg of 7th and every foll 8th row until there are 53 [55: 58: 60: 63] sts, taking inc sts into double moss st.

Cont straight until left front matches back to beg of armhole shaping, ending with RS facing for next row.

Shape armhole

Keeping patt correct, cast off 5 [6: 6: 7: 7] sts at beg of next row. 48 [49: 52: 53: 56] sts.

Work 1 row.

Dec 1 st at armhole edge of next 3 [3: 5: 5: 7] rows, then on foll 3 alt rows, then on every foll 4th row until 40 [41: 42: 43: 44] sts rem.

Cont straight until 15 [15: 15: 17: 17] rows less have been worked than on back to beg of shoulder shaping, ending with **WS** facing for next row.

Shape neck

Keeping patt correct, cast off 9 [10: 10: 10: 10] sts at beg of next row. 31 [31: 32: 33: 34] sts.

Dec 1 st at neck edge of next 6 rows, then on foll 2 [2: 2: 3: 3] alt rows, then on foll 4th row, ending with RS facing for next row. 22 [22: 23: 23: 24] sts.

Shape shoulder

Cast off 7 [7: 8: 8: 8] sts at beg of next and foll alt row.

Work 1 row.

Cast off rem 8 [8: 7: 7: 8] sts.

RIGHT FRONT

Using 4mm (US 6) needles cast on 38 [40: 43: 45: 48] sts.

Row 1 (RS): K2, *K2, P2, rep from * to last 0 [2: 1: 3: 2] sts, K0 [2: 1: 2: 2], P0 [0: 0: 1: 0].

Row 2: P0 [0: 1: 0: 0], K2 [0: 2: 1: 0], *P2, K2, rep from * to end.

These 2 rows form rib.

Cont in rib for a further 19 rows, ending with **WS** facing for next row.

Row 22 (WS): Rib 11 [13: 16: 18: 21], (M1, rib 2) 3 times, M1, rib 7, M1, rib 3, M1, rib 7, (M1, rib 2) twice. 46 [48: 51: 53: 56] sts.

Change to 4½mm (US 7) needles.

Beg and ending rows as indicated, cont in patt

from chart for body and complete to match left front, reversing shapings, working an extra row before beg of armhole, neck and shoulder shaping.

SLEEVES

Using 4mm (US 6) needles cast on 50 [50: 52: 54: 54] sts.

Row 1 (RS): K0 [0: 1: 2: 2], P2, *K2, P2, rep from * to last 0 [0: 1: 2: 2] sts, K0 [0: 1: 2: 2].

Row 2: P0 [0: 1: 2: 2], K2, *P2, K2, rep from * to last 0 [0: 1: 2: 2] sts, P0 [0: 1: 2: 2].

These 2 rows form rib.

Cont in rib for a further 19 rows, ending with **WS** facing for next row.

Row 22 (WS): Rib 15 [15: 16: 17: 17], M1, rib 2, M1, rib 7, M1, rib 3, M1, rib 7, M1, rib 2, M1, rib to last st, inc in last st. 57 [57: 59: 61: 61] sts.

Change to 4½mm (US 7) needles.

Beg and ending rows as indicated and repeating the 24 row patt repeat throughout, cont in patt from chart for sleeve, shaping sides by inc 1 st at each end of 11th [9th: 11th: 11th: 9th] and every foll 14th [12th: 12th: 12th: 10th] row to 69 [71: 73: 75: 73] sts, then on every foll - [-: -: -: 12th] row until there are - [-: -: -: 77] sts, taking inc sts into double moss st.

Cont straight until sleeve meas 45 [45: 46: 46: 46] cm, ending with RS facing for next row.

Sleeve chart

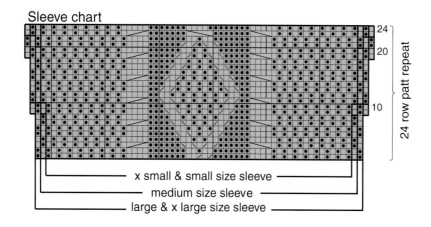

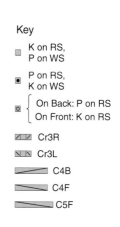

24 row patt repeat

x small & small size sleeve

medium size sleeve

large & x large size sleeve

Key

K on RS, P on WS

P on RS, K on WS

{ On Back: P on RS
On Front: K on RS

Cr3R

Cr3L

C4B

C4F

C5F

Shape top

Keeping patt correct, cast off 5 [6: 6: 7: 7] sts at beg of next 2 rows. 59 [59: 61: 61: 63] sts.
Dec 1 st at each end of next 3 rows, then on foll 3 alt rows, then on every foll 4th row until 41 [41: 43: 43: 45] sts rem.
Work 1 row, ending with RS facing for next row.
Dec 1 st at each end of next and every foll alt row to 31 sts, then on foll 5 rows, ending with RS facing for next row.
Cast off rem 21 sts, dec 4 sts evenly.

MAKING UP

Press as described on the information page.
Join shoulder seams using back stitch, or mattress stitch if preferred.

Collar

With RS facing and using 4mm (US 6) needles, beg and ending at front opening edges, pick up and knit 24 [25: 25: 26: 28] sts up right side of neck, 26 [28: 28: 30: 30] sts from back, then 24 [25: 25: 26: 28] sts down left side of neck. 74 [78: 78: 82: 86] sts.

Row 1 (WS): K4, *P2, K2, rep from * to last 2 sts, K2.
Row 2: K2, *P2, K2, rep from * to end.
These 2 rows form rib.
Cont in rib until collar meas 16 cm, ending with RS facing for next row.

Cast off in rib.
See information page for finishing instructions, setting in sleeves using the set-in method. Insert zip into front opening, positioning top of zip pull 7 cm up from collar pick-up row. Fold collar in half to inside and slip stitch in place.

53 [54: 55: 56: 57] cm
(21 [21.5: 21.5: 22: 22.5] in)

46.5 [48.5: 51.5: 53.5: 57] cm
(18.5 [19: 20.5: 21: 22.5] in)

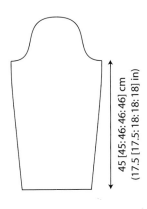

45 [45: 46: 46: 46] cm
(17.5 [17.5: 18: 18: 18] in)

 ## Harris

YARN

	XS-S	M	L-XL	
To fit bust	81-86	91	97-102	cm
	32-34	36	38-40	in

RYC Cashsoft Aran

	12	13	14	x 50gm

(photographed in Oat 001)

NEEDLES

1 pair 4mm (no 8) (US 6) needles
1 pair 4½mm (no 7) (US 7) needles
4mm (no 8) (US 6) circular needle

TENSION

19 sts and 25 rows to 10 cm measured over stocking stitch using 4½mm (US 7) needles.

CENTRE PANELS (make 2)

Using 4mm (US 6) needles cast on 89 [95: 101] sts.
Row 1 (RS): K1, *P1, K1, rep from * to end.
Row 2: As row 1.
These 2 rows form moss st.
Work in moss st for a further 24 rows, ending with RS facing for next row.
Change to 4½mm (US 7) needles.
Beg with a K row, cont in st st until centre panel meas 30 [31: 32] cm, ending with RS facing for next row.
Dec 1 st at each end of next and every foll 6th row to 75 [81: 87] sts, then on every foll 4th row to 53 [63: 73] sts, then on every foll alt row until 35 [37: 39] sts rem.

Work 1 row, ending with RS facing for next row.
Cast off.

SIDE PANELS (make 2)

Using 4mm (US 6) needles cast on 45 [49: 53] sts.
Work in moss st as given for centre panel for 26 rows, ending with RS facing for next row.
Change to 4½mm (US 7) needles.
Beg with a K row, cont in st st until side panel meas 30 [31: 32] cm, ending with RS facing for next row.
Dec 1 st at each end of next and every foll 8th row to 27 [37: 47] sts, then on every foll 6th row until 17 [19: 21] sts rem.
Work 5 rows, ending with RS facing for next row.
Cast off.

MAKING UP

Press as described on the information page.
Noting that "side seams" fall centrally up side panels, join centre panels to side panels using back stitch, or mattress stitch if preferred, and leaving 15 cm openings in side front seams, beg 15 cm up from cast-on edge.

Opening borders (both alike)
With RS facing and using 4mm (US 6) needles, pick up and knit 29 sts along side panel row-end edge of opening.
Work in moss st as given for centre panel for 9 rows, ending with RS facing for next row.
Cast off in moss st.
Sew ends of borders in place on RS of centre panel.

Collar

With RS facing and using 4mm (US 6) circular needle, pick up and knit 96 [104: 112] sts evenly all round neck edge.
Round 1 (RS): *K1, P1, rep from * to end.
Round 2 (RS): *P1, K1, rep from * to end.
These 2 rounds form moss st.
Cont in moss st for a further 36 rounds, ending with RS facing for next row.
Cast off in moss st.
Fold collar in half to outside and slip st in place.
See information page for finishing instructions.

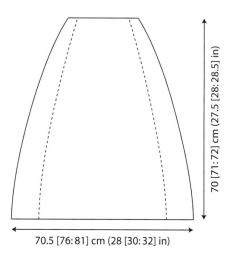

70 [71: 72] cm (27.5 [28: 28.5] in)

70.5 [76: 81] cm (28 [30: 32] in)

BELGIUM
Pavan, Meerlaanstraat 73,
B9860 Balegem (Oosterzele).
Tel: (32) 9 221 8594
Email: pavan@pandora.be

CANADA
Diamond Yarn,
9697 St Laurent,
Montreal,
Quebec, H3L 2N1.
Tel: (514) 388 6188

Diamond Yarn (Toronto),
155 Martin Ross,
Unit 3, Toronto,
Ontario,M3J 2L9.
Tel: (416) 736 6111
Email: diamond@diamondyarn.com
Web: www.diamondyarns.com

DENMARK
Design Vaerkstedet,
Boulevarden 9, 9000 Aalborg.
Tel: (45) 9812 0713
Fax: (45) 9813 0213

Inger's, Volden 19, 8000 Aarhus.
Tel: (45) 8619 4044

Sommerfuglen, Vandkunsten 3,
1467 Kobenhavn k.
Tel/Fax: (45) 3332 8290
Email: mail@sommerfuglen.dk
Web: www.sommerfuglen.dk

Uldstedet, Fiolstraede 13,
1171 Kobenhavn k.
Tel/Fax: (45) 3391 1771

Uldstedet, G1. Jernbanevej 7,
2800 Lyngby.
Tel/Fax: (45) 4588 1088

Garnhokeren,
Karen Olsdatterstraede 9, 4000 Roskilde.
Tel/Fax: (45) 4637 2063

FINLAND
Oy Nordia Produkter Ab,
Mikkolantie 1,
00640 Helsinki.
Tel: (358) 9 777 4272
Email: info@nordiaprodukter.fi

FRANCE
Elle Tricot : 8 Rue du Coq,
67000 Strasbourg.
Tel: (33) 3 88 23 03 13.
Email: elletricot@agat.net.
Web: www.elletricote.com

GERMANY
Wolle & Design,
Wolfshovener Strasse 76,
52428 Julich-Stetternich.
Tel: (49) 2461 54735.
Email: Info@wolleunddesign.de.
Web: www.wolleunddesign.de

HOLLAND
de Afstap, Oude Leliestraat 12,
1015 AW Amsterdam.
Tel: (31) 20 6231445

HONG KONG
East Unity Co Ltd, Unit B2, 7/F Block B,
Kailey Industrial Centre,
12 Fung Yip Street, Chai Wan.
Tel: (852) 2869 7110
Fax: (852) 2537 6952
Email: eastuni@netvigator.com

ICELAND
Storkurinn, Laugavegi 59,
101 Reykjavik.
Tel: (354) 551 8258
Fax: (354) 562 8252
Email: malin@mmedia.is

ITALY
D.L. srl, Via Piave, 24 – 26,
20016 Pero, Milan.
Tel: (39) 02 339 10 180.

JAPAN
Puppy Co Ltd, T151-0051,
3-16-5 Sendagaya, Shibuyaku, Tokyo.
Tel: (81) 3 3490 2827
Email: info@rowan-jaeger.com

KOREA
Coats Korea Co Ltd,
5F Kuckdong B/D,
935-40 Bangbae-Dong,
Seocho-Gu, Seoul.
Tel: (82) 2 521 6262.
Fax: (82) 2 521 5181

NORWAY
Coats Norge A/S,
Postboks 63, 2801 Gjovik.
Tel: (47) 61 18 34 00
Fax: (47) 61 18 34 20

SINGAPORE
Golden Dragon Store,
101 Upper Cross Street #02-51,
People's Park Centre.
Singapore 058357
Tel: (65) 65358454.
Email:gdscraft@hotmail.com

SOUTH AFRICA
Arthur Bales PTY,
PO Box 44644,
Linden 2104.
Tel: (27) 11 888 2401.

SPAIN
Oyambre, Pau Claris 145,
80009 Barcelona.
Tel: (34) 670 011957.
Email: comercial@oyambreonline.com

SWEDEN
Wincent, Norrtullsgatan 65,
113 45 Stockholm.
Tel: (46) 8 33 70 60
Fax: (46) 8 33 70 68
Email: wincent@chello.se
Web: www.wincentyarn.com

TAIWAN
Laiter Wool Knitting Co Ltd,
10-1 313 Lane, Sec 3,
Chung Ching North Road,
Taipei.
Tel: (886) 2 2596 0269.

Long T eh Trading Co Ltd,
3F No. 19-2,
Kung Yuan Road,
Taichung.
Tel: (886) 4 2225 6698.

Green Leave Thread Company,
No 181, Sec 4,
Chung Ching North Road,
Taipei.
Fax: (886) 2 8221 2919.

U.S.A.
Westminster Fibers Inc,
4 Townsend West,
Suite 8, Nashua,
New Hampshire 03063.
Tel: (1 603) 886 5041 / 5043.
Email: rowan@westminsterfibers.com

U.K.
Rowan, Green Lane Mill,
Holmfirth, West Yorkshire,
HD9 2DX.
Tel: 01484 681881.
Email: mail@ryclassic.com
Web: www.ryclassic.com

For All Other Countries:
Please contact Rowan for stockists details.

Shot on Location in and around Golspie
and Brora, Sutherland and Portmahomack,
Easter Ross, Scotland.

With enormous thanks to:
Lord Strathnaver, The Sutherland Estate
Bunny Crabtree, Backies
The Royal Marine Hotel, Brora
Golspie Golf Club
Tarbat Ness Visitor Centre
Blanche Sinclair, Golspie

Photographer Mark Scott (assisted By
Rachel Whiting and Katie Hyams)
Stylist – Tara Sloggett
Make up – KJ
Models – Rosie Tasker and Sara Faulkner
Design layout – Nicky Downes

First published in Great Britain in 2005
by Rowan Yarns Ltd, Green Lane Mill,
Holmfirth, West Yorkshire, England, HD9 2DX

British Library Cataloguing in
Publication Data
Rowan Yarns
RYC Weekend
ISBN 1-904485-47-2